Praise the Lord for He is good;
sing to our God for He is loving:
to Him our praise is due.
Psalm 147:1-11

PRAYER, FAITH AND A BIT OF CHOCOLATE

Stories of Everyday Miracles

by Rosemarie Gortler
Diane Carroll Vogel
Sallie Bachar

First printing, May, 2009
© 2009 Rosemarie Gortler,
Diane Carroll Vogel
and Sallie Bachar

Printed in the United States. All rights reserved.

ISBN: 978-0-9795394-6-6

Father's Press

Lee's Summit, MO
(816) 600-6288
www.fatherspress.com
E-Mail: fatherspress@yahoo.com

Prayer, Faith and a Bit of Chocolate

Introduction

The stories in this book are about prayer and trust in God. Turning to God in everyday living and especially in difficult times, acknowledges our trust in Him and our complete dependence on Him.

God answers our prayers in the manner He believes will serve us best. Sometimes, the answer is hard to understand, especially when the answer given is not what was asked for. But—*in due time*, our Merciful Savior always gives us more and better than we prayed for. Have faith that He listens. Prayers are always answered.

Remember that with God's help, we can also help ourselves. We can indulge in the God-given comforts of Earth. It's possible to minimize stress by practicing deep breathing, by walking for exercise, and by talking with family and friends. And—it helps to partake in a bite—or a bit more—of His "Divinely Delicious" chocolate for comfort. Chocolate delivers a bunch of antioxidants and feel-good chemicals to the brain as well as comfort to the taste buds. We bet that God approves of using a bit of His chocolate to help us out! So—we added favorite recipes for chocolate comfort between the stories.

Pray a lot. Trust God. And—it's O.K. to have a bite of God's comfort-giving chocolate now and again.

Then, don't forget to give praise and thanksgiving for His blessings.

God bless you,
Rosemarie, Diane and Sallie

Table of Contents

Laura's Gift   1
When a grandmother's two-year-old grandchild died, it took her son's faith for her to see the gifts the family had been given.

I Hear You Calling from Above   9
A seven-year old's 104 degree temperature dropped dramatically, allowing him to hold his grieving grandmother's hand as they walked to his beloved grandfather's burial site.

Wake-up Call   13
The gifts of the Holy Spirit allow us to make a difference in the lives of others in small ways as well as in big and exciting ways.

A Chocolate Cake that Beats Allergies   17

My Angel Left a Calling Card   19
Carolyn asked for God's help when a deer smashed into her car. Her shoes and all the contents of the car flew out the shattered windows, but her blessed angel auto clip was intact.

Tuesday's Child   23
Prayer helped this mother cope with fear after she overheard the nurse express concern about a knot in the umbilical cord during her baby's delivery.

And the Blind Shall See   27
Ted was accidentally blinded by a BB gun. Praise God for the miracle of sight in one eye.

Beat Stress with Tasty Antioxidants   32

Five Kids and a Dog   33
With tears and sobbing, the children prayed that their runaway puppy would find her way home. That was unlikely but....

A Mother's Undying Love   39
A grief stricken daughter receives comfort from an unexpected gift which she received shortly after her mother's death.

The Holy Spirit Even Helps With Housework   43
A death in the family, a frightening diagnosis and a grandchild's emergency surgery—all happening over a few days— were overwhelming. Talking to the Holy Spirit proved to be calming and allowed a formerly impossible task to be accomplished.

Relax and make a batch of mint chocolate brownies.   47

Thank You Lord   49
A teen's prayer during a near fatal accident is a reflection of a prayer she wrote for her First Holy Communion when she asked God to watch over her always.

And He Sent His Angels   53
Rick's fainting episodes came without warning. Fatigue and exhaustion were constant companions. Doctors called it stress, until he almost died. Angels saved his life.

Apple Blossoms in September   57
An unusual phenomenon in nature took place as God called His faithful servant home.

Worried? Pray, then, indulge in the comfort of Ann's Chocolate Trifle.   62

Surviving Stress with Smiles, Hugs, Laughs and Chocolate   63

And Nicholas Lived   65
The doctors were pessimistic. But Nicholas felt God's presence and assured his Mom and the doctors that he would be healed—and he was.

The Good Samaritan   69
The return of a lost checkbook demonstrated the extraordinary power that both prayer and simple

kindness have in our everyday lives.

The Mascara Sign   73
An angry, newly divorced mother of two small children became cynical about life. It took a Divine message and a subsequent startling event to change her attitude.

Emergency Relief for Chocolate Cravings   77

A Belated Birthday   79
A new grandmother, expecting to celebrate her fiftieth birthday by rejoicing at the birth of her first grandchild, instead found herself at a hospital hundreds of miles from home.

Mail Order Message   85
God does work in mysterious ways. This time He used the Post Office!

Mary Told Me—Susie's O.K   89
A grieving mother's plea to the Blessed Virgin was answered.

Share chocolate pie with the funny crust with your inner child.   92

Paul's Joy   93
Paul's attitude toward the end of his life was surprising as well as unexpected. "I feel like a kid waiting for Christmas."

Elizabeth and the Irish Priest   101
Who was the priest with the Irish brogue and the bushy beard who came in to comfort us—the one that the chaplain insisted was not part of his staff?

Savor the heavenly aroma and taste of Baked Fudge Pudding Cake.   105

Wrapped in Prayer   107
A mother's hug and a man's incredible recovery are cloaked in love.

Anastasia and Nana, God's Rescue Squad   111
A vivid dream revealed to Marigrace the exact location of a lost surprise gift lovingly stitched to cheer her sister.

A Final Quick Chocolate Fix—and—   114
The Best Recipe of All

Acknowledgements   115

Authors   116

Laura's Gift

Rosemarie Gortler

"Near the cross of Jesus there stood his mother."
(John 19:25)

    Someone once said that a good stretch is worth an hour sleep.
    I don't know about that—but a good stretch felt good on that November morning. My husband and I were visiting our son, daughter-in-law and grandchildren in Colorado Springs. It was early—before 6 A.M. The house was quiet. I sat on the couch alternately stretching and sipping my steaming cup of coffee.

I love being alone for just a little while in the early hours. That's probably a result of having five children and very little time for uninterrupted thoughts. I had just enough of that quiet time when I heard my son quietly talking to our new grandson as he brought the baby down to me. I was delighted. His mom had fed him. He was full, happy and playful.

Frederick William IV—his name is longer than he is.

The baby grinned up at me and responded to my peek-a-boo play with real belly laughs. We did the "so big" game and he thought clapping hands was a great way to spend time. We were having a wonderful time. Five months is such a cute age, but then, every age is cute to grandparents.

We played for a good while in the quiet of the morning. After a time he began rubbing his eyes. I responded to his tired message by positioning him with his head on my shoulder. Humming softly into his ear I began a rocking motion. In short time he was asleep.

I leaned back allowing myself the continuing pleasure of those precious moments as I enjoyed the warmth of his rhythmic breathing on my neck.

My thoughts drifted to the day before and some small talk with little Freddy's mother, my daughter-in-law Ellen. We were talking about Freddy and how active he was. We laughed about how little boys differ from little girls. Ellen noticed that boys bang things to make noise "just for the sound of noise." She remembered our granddaughters being more sedate in their play. I smiled, remembering that as babies, my three daughters were able to pass down their playpens in great shape but our two sons demolished their playpens.

Ellen's expression had changed. She looked intense as she changed the subject to mention her hope that her Laura would not be forgotten. Her comment startled me because we frequently talk about Laura Elizabeth. Laura "Liz," as I liked to call my granddaughter was two and a half when she died.

Memories flooded my mind....

    Laura was a tiny, delicate little girl. Her deep blue eyes were like her daddy's. She had soft sandy hair, which her sisters liked to comb and arrange. Laura was a "special" child who suffered seizures—sometimes one after the other—until your heart broke as you watched her suffer. But she had improved so much and the suffering had subsided following her last hospitalization.

    Laura... when she was pain free, had a gaze that seemed to say she needed you, trusted you and was relying on your gentleness. When you held her in your arms you responded to that gaze. I thought this was my own private thought until I watched my brother hold her the Christmas Eve before she died. He plays with children but just doesn't hold babies! Yet he held her for a long time that evening, looking at her with contentment and peace.

    My most vivid memory will forever be that of watching my husband at Laura's hospital crib side stroking her head as he told her that he would always be there to care for her. Laura drew out his love so completely, which in turn magnified my feelings towards him. Laura....

    When Laura was born I was devastated at the thought that she would never get to ride a bike or to run and play. The pain was not only for Laura but also for our son, for Ellen, and for the suffering they would experience because Laura would suffer. I was also caught up in Laura not meeting society's standards and how the world would treat her. That devastation slowly changed to a determination to help her to accomplish everything and anything she could be taught to accomplish and to help provide for her future.

    I held little Freddy tightly as my mind replayed the events of March 16, 1991, the day Laura died.

<p style="text-align:center">~~~</p>

It was 6:45 when the phone rang.

"Fred called at 5:00 this morning. He's on his way home and he wants the mother of all parties. I told him that everyone would be at the airport to greet him at 5:00 this afternoon."

My daughter-in-law, Ellen, spoke excitedly as she described the yellow ribbons which she and a friend tied to every tree that lined the street from the main highway along the several blocks to their home. She went over the menu for the party which was planned for Fred's return from the Gulf War. I assured her that I would bring a few salads and that we would leave our home at noon to make the two-hour trip to their home and then to the airport.

I could not stop grinning. I was giddy as I prepared coleslaw. I imagined Fred deplaning. For so many months my husband and I sat up until all hours of the night watching the war on TV. Our hearts were heavy when casualties were mentioned. We were as frightened as everyone else who had a loved one over there.

But Fred was coming home now. I looked at my watch—it was 7:00 A.M. Thoughts about Fred, Ellen and the three children reuniting were flooding my mind. Their children, our grandchildren, were 8, 6 and 2 years old at that time. Julie is the oldest, with Carolyn in the middle and Laura as the family inspiration.

Laura was born with a chromosomal abnormality and had been hospitalized many times in her two years. During those times, Ellen never left her side except when Fred came to relieve her. Together, they never forgot Julie and Carolyn's needs. Julie and Carolyn knew their way around Walter Reed Army Hospital almost as well as they knew their own home. They would show us where the candy machine was, lead us to the elevators and take us to the cafeteria.

Laura was a little fighter. She made it through those crisis times and had been doing so well for quite a while. I smiled as I imagined Fred once again jogging through the park pushing little

Laura Liz in the three-wheel jogging stroller while Julie and Carolyn rode their bikes along side. When your child is so sick, one smile will make your day. Fred and Ellen worked so hard for that smile. When Laura smiled, they glowed. I later discovered how common this is among parents of special children. Laura's disabilities were accepted and Laura was loved. She was a gift sent to inspire our entire family.

Now Laura was doing well and Fred was on his way home. He could jog in the park with his girls again. I chuckled as I went over Ellen's call and her excitement. What a day! Thank You Lord!

The phone rang. The clock said almost 8:00 A.M. It was Judi, our daughter living in Illinois. Judi and her family would be the only missing family members at this party. I was expecting her call. Judi would probably be lamenting her absence.

I was not prepared for her dismissal of my greeting. "Mom, something is wrong at Ellen's house—what is it?" I attempted to assure her that I had spoken with Ellen earlier and that all was well. "Mom—listen to me. Something is wrong. There's a baby sitter there and she tells me that Ellen isn't available. She wouldn't let me talk to the girls. Something happened. You and dad better get up there—now."

I quickly hung up and called Ellen. The baby-sitter answered and wouldn't allow me to talk to my grandchildren. I pleaded, "Please-I'm the grandmother and I might be needed. Did something happen to Laura?" She was quiet. "Should I come now?" She gave the phone to her husband and he simply told me that we should come early.

We left immediately. Somehow my husband and I knew that the situation was ominous. The trip was an interminable blur. Our hearts ached for Laura and for our son, for our daughter-in- law and for our granddaughters.

Our fears were real. When we arrived, Ellen was back home from the hospital emergency room. She was in shock. Her baby was dead. The death of a child is unnatural. Parents and certainly grandparents are supposed to precede children out of this world.

Ellen honored our request to go to the hospital to be with Laura for a few minutes. She called to tell the hospital staff that we would be coming to say "goodbye" to our little Laura Liz. We were told to meet the nurse in the chapel.

Within minutes, we were seated in the chapel awaiting the nurse. The nurse arrived carrying Laura, wrapped in a receiving blanket. That "angel of mercy" was as compassionate as can be as she offered us an opportunity to hold Laura and to be alone with her. Laura looked so sweet and so peaceful. We cried, kissed her still warm forehead and asked that she now pray for us. I never thought to ask the nurse's name but I still offer a prayer of thanks for her understanding.

The ride from the hospital back to Ellen's seemed never to end. But we got there. We leaned on each other. The phone kept ringing and the blur continued. Ellen's family was coming. Judi was flying in from Illinois. Other siblings of Ellen and Fred somehow got there. It was 11:00 A.M. now and getting harder to focus on anything.

I wished I could ease the pain reflected on Ellen's face. My husband's eyes were vacant. Ellen's parents looked pained. People spoke to me and I think I spoke back. I remember that it was 4:00 PM. We would have to leave for the airport soon.

The entire family started out to meet Fred at the airport. It was decided that Fred's dad, Ellen and the girls would go to the plane to meet him while the rest of us stayed in the private room given to us by the airport personnel.

My husband later told me that Fred's first words were, "Where's Laura?" When Fred came into the room where we were, he seemed to be in a trance. What could any of us say? We simply hugged.

Family members supported each other that night. It was another blur. We ate what was supposed to be party food. I can't recall any conversations. We all just "were." We only said what had to be said, but I felt close to the others in the sometimes stark silence. We were grieving. I went down to the basement to wash some clothes. It seemed important to just do something. Nothing else made sense.

All I could think about was how angry I was at God. How could He do such a thing? What cruelty. What an untimely thing for Him to do. My angry feelings continued throughout the sadness of the following day. I hollered and screamed at God under my breath.

The continuing blur makes it hard to remember the sequence of events. I remember ironing Laura's dress at some point. My husband and I and Ellen's parents went to choose the tiny white casket. I remember being in a flower shop. Somehow, we functioned in that blur. Somehow, we were at the funeral home the next day. Friends were coming and going.

I hugged Fred and sat him down to talk. I shared my anger at God with my son. I went on and on about how God's timing was incredibly bad. "How could He do this? What timing. On the day you come home. At 5:00 yesterday morning you spoke with your wife and thanked God for your homecoming and at 5:00 that same afternoon you came home to be told your daughter had died."

His response was simple. No, Mom, God's timing was good. What if God had taken Laura when I was away? I might not have been able to get back quickly. He waited until I was on my way. He wanted Laura but he took care of Ellen and the girls. I thank Him for that." His eyes were so sad. He hugged me.

I breathed deeply. He was right. Fred's faith helped me to lean on rather than to yell at God.

~~~

The sounds of the other children stirring upstairs brought me out of the memory trance. Little Freddy was still asleep on my shoulder. Somehow I knew that Laura knew my thoughts and that she was prayerfully smiling at God's gifts to us.

I thank God for my son's faith that allowed me to begin the healing which will never be complete—but becomes more tolerable as time goes by.

I thank God for family members. Together we weathered a storm which brought me closer to those with whom I could pour out my heart, yell at, become irritated with, pray with, grieve with and finally, lean on. God gave us family to love. Laura magnified that love. Laura taught us how important each of us is. Laura reminded us that love is giving—one to the other.

I often remind our other grandchildren that they have a cousin in heaven to pray for them. I feel Laura's presence often, especially at family functions. I felt her presence when her brother Freddy was born. I felt her there at the birth of her youngest cousin two months later.

Yes! Laura is around me a lot. Forget Laura? Never. And Laura hasn't forgotten us. Laura's gift is precious. She taught us all how strong love is and how love transcends life on earth.

I Hear You Calling From Above

Diane Carroll Vogel

*"Only in God be at rest, my soul,
for from Him comes my hope."*
(Psalm 62:6)

Our seven-year-old son, Doug, was struggling to breathe and his little body was limp. He looked up at me with glazed, blue eyes. Gently I brushed back his damp hair and stroked his hot forehead. Kneeling beside his bed, I agonized over what I considered a dreadful dilemma.

My father-in-law was to be buried today. Frank Vogel was a

kind and loving man who treated me like a daughter. I wanted to attend his funeral. He was also a wonderful grandfather. Doug would be upset if he missed this last opportunity to tell Granddaddy good-bye.

I could try to find a baby sitter, but Doug was too ill to leave in someone else's care. My husband, Tom, and our five-year-old daughter, Christine, would have to go without us. Yet, as Tom and Christine pulled out of the driveway, a strange sense of urgency overwhelmed me. Was there a special reason why Doug should be at the funeral, a reason beyond saying good-bye to his grandfather?

Tears streamed down my face. Then I remembered something a friend once told me. "Diane," she said, "when you face a dilemma or conflict, sit quietly by yourself and listen for God's answer." Was God trying to tell me something?

Kneeling beside Doug's bed once again, I placed my wrist against his feverish forehead for a moment before taking his temperature. The thermometer registered 104 degrees. My heart ached for my sleeping child. His breathing was labored, and his face was flushed.

Doug definitely needed to be taken to the doctor, but I would follow my friend's advice first. God would surely hear my silent plea for help. Closing my eyes, I remained silent and waited for spiritual direction.

Several seconds passed. Then out of the stillness came words I never expected to hear, and which to this day I cannot fully explain. Doug sat up and calmly said, "I am with you. I am going." The strange words he spoke did not sound like those a child would use.

I was stunned, but at the same time, filled with inner peace. Doug no longer looked sick. He was breathing easily. His cheeks were losing their burning glow and his eyes were no longer glazed. This time when I took his temperature, it registered as normal. His fever had broken!

Could we make it in time to his grandfather's funeral? We dressed quickly and completed the hour drive to my mother-in-law's house just as the family was leaving for a funeral mass to be held in the chapel at Fort Meyer. But this amazing story does not end here. Little Doug still had an important role to play in the day's events.

Dad Vogel, a retired Marine Corps colonel, was to be buried with full military honors. The funeral procession, which started at the chapel steps, wound solemnly through the sacred grounds of Arlington National Cemetery. I was moved by such an inspiring sight. My strongest memory, however, is an image of my small son and his distraught grandmother at the burial site itself.

After the mourners got out of their cars, they lined up for the final part of the memorial service. My mother-in-law, Ann, was assigned a military escort. This young Marine was impressive in his full dress uniform and respectful in his manner. He held out his arm for her to take and they started walking.

Tom, our two children, and I followed with the rest of the family and the other mourners behind Ann and her Marine escort. I noticed how straight my mother-in-law's back was as she walked. Her outward composure was dignified and beautiful. But Frank was the love of her life, the man she called her best friend, and she was devastated by his unexpected death from a heart attack at the age of 62.

How dreadfully lonely she must have felt at that moment, especially with no one from her family beside her. Suddenly, without prodding from anyone, little Doug pulled away from us and moved to his grandmother's side. He placed his small hand in hers, and her fingers closed gratefully around it. Grandmother and Grandson, they walked hand in hand to the gravesite.

Once again, my heart filled with awe and wonder. "I am with you. I am going." Were those really Doug's words? Was someone else also walking beside Ann Vogel when Doug grasped her hand? I like to think that Frank reached out to his grief-stricken wife through their grandson. I also believe that Jesus, who loves little children, sent Doug to comfort his grandmother.

My son, who is now 33, remembers only fragments of this incident, but I have told him the story often and he does not tire of hearing it. From time to time, my mother-in-law and I also reminisce about this remarkable event, and it still amazes and moves us.

Trauma and tragedy touch all of our lives. We seek solace from family and friends. We cry out to God, and when our prayers are answered, we rejoice. If our despair and pain continue, we wonder if Heaven has turned a deaf ear to our pleas. Yet, endless stories, like those of little Doug and his grandmother, testify to God's great love and compassion. The following verse from David Hass' "You Are Mine" holds special meaning on occasions such as this.

I will come to you in the silence.
I will lift you from all your fear.
You will hear my voice, I claim you as my choice,
Be still and know I am here.

God holds us in His heart and hears us when we call to Him, but sometimes He requires us to listen in silence for His answer.

Wake-up Call

Sallie Bachar

"Now there are varieties of gifts, but the same Spirit...."
(1 Cor. 12:4)

    The phone rang at 11:00 p.m. Too late for a social call. Intuition told me something was wrong.

    "Sal," my sister said, "I'm at the hospital again with Dennis, but we'll be okay. You don't have to come. I just thought I would let you know."

    "Are you sure you don't want me to come?" I asked.

    "No, we'll be fine," she assured me. I promised prayers and

told her to call in the morning.
   My brother-in-law, Dennis, had been in and out of the hospital for the past two months. The doctors diagnosed him with a degenerative heart condition, and, along with that, he had poor circulation throughout his body. His oxygen levels would plunge dangerously low, making it extremely difficult for him to breathe. After a few days of being hospitalized, however, he always perked up. This was just another one of those times I told myself. They would put him on oxygen, adjust his medication again and send him home in a couple of days.
   Jean sounded calm on the phone and she did tell me there was no need for me to come, so I settled back in my chair to finish watching the movie, but I couldn't concentrate.
   Sensing my uneasiness, my husband urged, "Why don't you get dressed and drive to the hospital? You know you will feel better if you go." He was right, and so I gave in to the nagging voice inside.
   I found my sister pacing in the waiting room. As soon as she caught sight of me, she ran into my arms and wept as I held her close. In the silence of that embrace I realized I was the answer to her unspoken prayer. I had a gift to share. In fact, I was the gift, and I shudder to think I almost withheld myself from her.
   God was working in both of us. She had a need. I could satisfy that need. My gift was simple. It touched only one person at one moment in time. To my sister, it meant the world. No other person could have comforted her as I did.
   St. Paul tells us, "There are different kinds of spiritual gifts but the same Spirit; there are different forms of service but the same Lord; there are different workings but the same God who produces all of them in everyone. To each individual the manifestation of the Spirit is given for some benefit."
(1 Cor. 12:4-7)
   After reading that passage and the following verses

describing the specific gifts of the Spirit, I always wondered what gifts, if any, I had been given. Then I would sigh and think, *No, not me. Those gifts are for someone else. I'm just an ordinary woman, living an ordinary life.*

Deep down inside, however, the thought persisted that perhaps those words just might pertain to me too. I started to look for various ways I could make a difference in the lives of others, but I kept looking for something big and exciting, somewhere "out there," beyond the reach of my daily existence. While I was seeking some grand way to be used by God, He placed a need right before me. I already had the gift to share, even though I didn't realize it.

In one late-night phone call, God revealed that my simple presence alone was gift enough to be used in His kingdom.

Prayer, Faith and a Bit of Chocolate

A Chocolate Cake to Beat Allergies

Diane Carroll Vogel

My 18-month-old son, Doug, was diagnosed with dust, egg and milk allergies. I really had to watch his environment and his diet. Believe me, I shed numerous tears over this little boy and said many prayers for him. I found tasty recipes to delight him and stimulate his appetite. A favorite dessert was a distinctive cocoa cake that used no eggs or milk. It tasted rich and chocolaty, and I could make fanciful shapes for special occasions like birthdays. My prayers and faith helped me accept my child's condition, and unique recipes like this chocolate cake helped him feel special.

Beat 'n' Bake Chocolate Cake
1½ cups flour
¾ cup sugar
¼ cup unsweetened cocoa
1 teaspoon soda
½ teaspoon. salt
1 teaspoon vanilla
1 cup cold water
¼ cup oil
1 tablespoon vinegar

Grease the bottom of a cake pan (round or square). Combine the flour with the sugar, cocoa, soda and salt right in the pan. Blend in the vanilla, water, oil, and vinegar with a fork. Mix well. Bake at 350 degrees for 30-35 minutes, or until the top springs back when touched lightly in the center. When the cake is cool, top it with your favorite frosting or whipped topping. Make enough batter for two pans, if you want a two-layer cake.

My Angel Left a Calling Card

Rosemarie Gortler

As told by Carolyn Gortler

"...I will strengthen you, I will help you, I will uphold you with my victorious right hand."
(Isaiah 41:10)

Rain was coming down in buckets, but my step had a bounce and warm, fuzzy feelings put a song on my lips as I walked to my car. I was coming from what I thought was a great after-college- graduation- job interview in North Carolina.

Mom and Dad suggested that I stay at a hotel and drive back to Virginia the next day. But it was only 2:00 in the afternoon and I wanted to get back to college for class and an exam tomorrow. Visibility seemed OK. It would be easier to get the exam over with and not miss the class material.

Darn! A flat tire. Oh well! A call to AAA assured me they would arrive shortly. But hours passed and still no Triple A. Annoyed at this, I shook my head and went back into the hotel and explained my dilemma to a bellhop. He helped me change into my spare tire so I could drive to the Firestone store to buy a new one.

With a brand new tire, I once again "hit the road" at about 5:00. I hate driving in the rain, especially at dusk or in the dark. But, determined to get back to school, I continued driving; all the while praying that God would help me to arrive home safely.

The car needed fuel and I was hungry so we both hurriedly "refueled" at South Hill, Virginia. Before getting back on the road, I called Dad and my sister, Julie, to tell them where I was and what I was doing.

Despite the tire setback, my mood was good again. The interview flashed back to mind. That helped calm the slight anxiety about my first experience of driving a long distance in an unfamiliar area in the dark. Once again I asked for Divine protection.

~~~

Suddenly, a huge white "thing" appeared from nowhere and slammed into my windshield. A cloud of dust filled the car. I felt like I was choking. The road was moving around me. I was being roughly jostled back and forth.

What was happening? I was in a time warp with sights separated from sounds. I felt around for my cell phone. It wasn't in the car. I finally realized that I was upside down. I kept praying. *"Please God, keep me safe. Help me."*

After releasing my seat belt, I must have fallen down to the car roof— but I don't recall falling or having any rational thought process about what I was doing at that time. My shoes were not on my feet. There was no glass in the windows, but that didn't seem strange. I managed to crawl out the window but felt disoriented standing there on the road. Later, the police told me what really happened but when it was happening I had no knowledge of hitting a deer or of my car skidding first on wheels, then flipping over and skidding on the roof. I wondered what was happening. I could only say over and over, *"Please God, help me."*

A kind lady stopped and took me into her car. She called my parents and my sister. A trucker stopped too. He called 911 and they took me to the hospital by ambulance. The ambulance personnel kept repeating their surprise at my surviving that wreck. I don't remember even looking at the wreck. I was numb and confused.

~~~

At the hospital, I was examined thoroughly, then observed for a few hours and discharged when my parents arrived. The time waiting for my parents was spent on the phone—talking to my grandparents and my sister. I didn't sustain a scratch and I wasn't feeling anxious and I was coherent and no longer confused. I was so grateful.

My parents and 10-year-old brother arrived at 11:30 that evening and our very tired family retired to the nearest motel. They didn't awaken me the next morning when they went to the towing company to look at the wreckage. My brother, Freddy, noticed the Guardian Angel auto visor clip in the car. The auto clip had been blessed and given to my sister and me from my grandparents to remind us to pray for safety. Freddy took it from the visor and later gave it to me.

In the morning we began the trip home, but first, Dad stopped at the accident site. Mom and Dad were horrified at the sight of a metal pole from the traffic sign which impaled the car inches away from the driver's side window. It was knocked out of its cement grounding and had stopped the car from skidding further.

Mom said she shivered when she saw how close that pole was to the driver's seat—barely missing me. Walking along the road, they picked up my scattered belongings from the ditch and from many feet in all directions. My belongings had been thrown from the car. The blessed angel clip held firmly to the visor. It had not been tossed out with my shoes, purse, phone and other items.

Mom and Dad considered my survival a miracle. Mom again repeated that she felt divinely protected. Both parents kept repeating gratitude for my survival—a litany of thanksgiving. Mom shivered, talking about what could have happened. Then, together, we prayed prayers of thanksgiving.

The police estimated that after hitting the deer, my car skidded 35 feet before flipping over and another 50 feet on the roof after the flip. The glass was gone from all the windows. I didn't have a scratch on my body—not even from climbing out the window with glass all around!

My parents had prayed that I would have a safe trip. I prayed along the way. God heard our prayers and our Good Lord sent an Angel to help.

My Guardian Angel left a calling card. When everything else was thrown out the windows, our intact Angel auto clip remained on the visor. We believe it was an Angelic calling card to remind us that God had heard our prayers for a safe trip!

Thank You Lord.

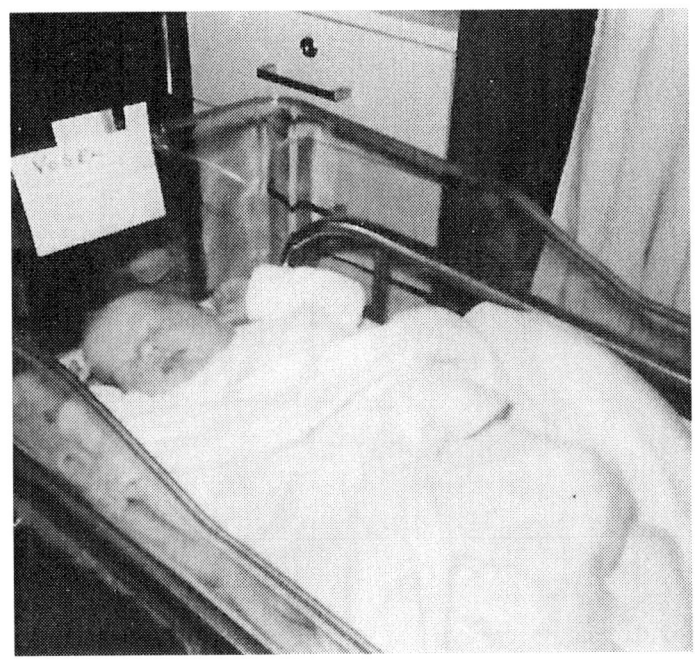

Tuesday's Child

Diane Carroll Vogel

"...happy is he who trusts in the Lord."
(Proverbs 16:20)

My obstetrician wanted to induce my labor early. Two weeks early in fact. By going along with his advice, did I save my baby's life, or jeopardize it? I will never know for sure. What I do know is that Christine was my miracle baby, and God was with her the day she was born.

I still remember my final office visit when the doctor suggested setting up a delivery date. I had misgivings at first. I had not dilated much yet and believed babies should go to full term. Moreover, the doctor offered no medical reasons for inducing labor early. However, he told me the baby was a good size already and a scheduled birth would be easier for all concerned. Of course, he added that my husband and I had to make the final decision.

When I returned home, my husband and I talked everything over. The doctor's reasons were not medically based, but they sounded logical. And, our baby would be with us in just a few days! We were thrilled.

Pushing all anxieties aside, I called my doctor and scheduled the delivery date. Then Tom and I notified our families and arranged for neighborhood friends to care for our 23-month-old son, Doug. I had finished decorating the nursery weeks ago and my hospital bag was packed. Except for last minute preparations, we were ready to bring our new baby home!

The night before Christine's birth, her daddy and I were so excited we had trouble sleeping. Finally, we gave up trying. We tried reading, but couldn't concentrate, so we sat up in bed and just talked. We also prayed together and asked our Lord to be with us when our baby was born.

The clock in our bedroom slowly ticked off the minutes, but at last, it was time to leave. Once we arrived at the hospital, things moved quickly. By 9:00 A.M., I was prepped for delivery and labor was induced. Tom would be with me during my labor and the baby's birth. His presence was a great comfort.

I was hooked up to a fetal monitor, and we watched it with increasing excitement. The monitor, which charted the progress of my contractions, assured us our baby was okay. My early contractions caused some discomfort, but were manageable. And my Tom was there to hold my hand.

We thought labor would take a long time—as it had with our first baby. Naturally, things often don't go as we expect. Within two hours, my contractions were coming fast and furious, faster than even the doctor had anticipated. Even worse, the epidural was working on one side of my body only. My labor pains were excruciating and exhausting.

I was more than ready for Baby to pop out. Evidently, Baby was just as ready. If memory serves me correctly, I screamed, "The baby's coming now!" My doctor, who was on his way to perform a C-section on another patient, was quickly summoned back to my bedside. Tom was abruptly ushered out, and I was rushed to the delivery room.

Things were happening so quickly, Tom was not allowed in the delivery room. At this point, however, all I cared about was my baby. I concentrated on breathing, pushing, and ignoring my pain. Marilyn, the nurse who attended me in the labor room, was also with me in the delivery room. She was not Tom, but she was a comforting angel indeed, and I welcomed her experienced and sensitive support.

By looking into a strategically placed mirror, I was able to watch Christine being born. Very few sights are as soul and heart stirring as the moment a woman becomes a mother, and I marveled over the miracle of my daughter's birth.

On July 15, 1975 at 11:45 A.M., Christine Carroll Vogel came yowling into the world. She weighed seven pounds two ounces and was nineteen and five eighths inches long. I had not known the sex of my baby before she was born, but I hoped I could give my son a little sister. When I heard the doctor call out, "It's a girl," I was ecstatic. When he placed her briefly on my chest, tears of delight trickled down my cheeks.

Once I was finally taken to the maternity room and Christine was brought to me, I studied her carefully. Her tiny head was perfectly shaped and unmarked by forceps. Her skin was clear and smooth. I undid her swaddling blanket and counted each of her slender fingers and toes. They were all there. She was the prettiest baby I had ever seen. I already had a darling little boy, and now I had my precious little girl. "Thank you, God," I whispered.

Holding my sleeping baby in my arms filled me with joy and gratitude. Then, a nagging thought shadowed my happiness. I remembered overhearing a delivery room nurse murmuring something in a low voice. The baby, she remarked, had a large knot in her umbilical chord. I had been concerned when I heard this, but shoved my anxiety aside when no one else seemed alarmed.

Now my uneasiness had returned. As soon as I could, I asked a maternity ward nurse if a knot in the umbilical chord could cause any long-range problems for my baby. She was reluctant to tell me much at first. When I insisted, she admitted this condition was a major cause of babies being stillborn, but assured me Christine was just fine.

Nonetheless, my anxiety persisted. What if Christine had gone to full term? Would her oxygen have been cut off? Or, did her umbilical chord become knotted after I was induced and active labor began? If Christine had died during delivery, whom could I blame? My doctor? Myself? Both of us?

It was useless to dwell on such thoughts. I looked down at the infant cradled in my arms. For a few seconds her eyelids fluttered open, and as I gazed into her slate blue eyes, my heart swelled with love. One way or the other, Christine was my miracle baby. I was so very grateful to God. According to an old nursery rhyme, "Tuesday's child is full of grace." The grace of God was with Christine the Tuesday she was born.

And the Blind Shall See

Sallie Bachar

"In all circumstances, give thanks, for this is the will of God for you in Christ Jesus."
(1Thessalonians 5:18)

    My husband, Ted, left the house just before dawn to meet his friend, Brian, for a day of partridge hunting. He promised he would be back by early afternoon in plenty of time for me to go shopping with our two-year old daughter, Terri.
    I spent the morning dusting and vacuuming the house, then made an early lunch so Terri could take her nap and be awake by the time Ted arrived home. Two o'clock passed. Then three.

Then four. It was a gloomy October day, and darkness was settling in quickly.

Shortly after four, the phone rang. I didn't recognize Brian's voice at first. "There's been an accident," he said. "Ted's been shot."

Panic seized my entire body. I couldn't grasp the words. He must have made a mistake. *It can't be! It can't be!* The words repeated themselves over and over in my head.

"I'm coming to get you," he said, "to take you to the hospital." I hung up the phone, still not believing what I had heard. Suddenly, I thought of Terri. I couldn't leave her alone nor could I take her with me. I called my mother. Ted had taken the car. My mother didn't drive, so she sent my sixteen-year old brother to get Terri. It was homecoming weekend, and although he had plans with his friends, he took the time to pick up his niece so my mother could baby-sit.

My next call was to Ted's mother. I had so little information, but she needed to know. She was as helpless as I was living on a country road ten miles away. Like my own mother, Ted's mother did not drive and depended upon neighbors and family to take her wherever she needed to go. I told her to pray and promised I would call as soon as I had more information.

It seemed like an eternity before Brian finally arrived. During the short drive to the hospital, he pieced the details of the accident together for me.

Brian told me that he and Ted were walking through very thick brush about fifty yards from one another when a partridge flew up between them. Brian turned and shot at the bird. Ted was in his direct line of fire, and hundreds of BBs penetrated his body. His upper chest and face took the brunt of the discharge.

He couldn't see but never lost consciousness. Brian led him out of the woods, but what usually would have taken twenty minutes to get to the road, took almost two hours because of

Ted's condition.

Brian tried to assure me Ted was going to be all right, but nothing he said prepared me for the shock of seeing him. His shirt was soaked in blood. His face was twice its normal size, and dotted with small wounds where the BBs entered. His eyes were swollen shut, and although he couldn't see, he knew I was there.

The doctors, concerned about his eyesight, were unable to deal with the seriousness of the injuries at our small facility. They sent him by ambulance to the nearest city fifteen miles south, where some of the best eye doctors in the state practiced.

I rode in the back of the ambulance by my husband's side. It seemed to take forever. By now, Ted was in a great deal of pain and vomiting blood. I was frightened and afraid he would die before we got to the hospital.

As soon as we arrived, the medical personnel whisked him away. While Ted was being prepped for surgery, I was answering a myriad of questions in the admissions office.

I had no idea where they had taken him or what was happening. A nurse escorted me from admissions to a darkened third floor waiting room. It was past eight o'clock and all visitors had left. Lights were dimmed in the hallways, and patients' doors were closed. The silence was deafening.

Another nurse approached and informed me that my husband was in surgery to remove the pellets from his upper body and that the most prominent eye surgeon in the entire state would perform the surgery to remove the BBs from his eyes. The doctor could make no guarantees, however. She said, "He may be blind."

I crumpled into the chair and sobbed. He was only 23 years old. We had a little child who was only two. Our life together was just beginning. How could this happen?

Blind—the word echoed through my mind over and over again as I tried to understand its implications.

The night duty nurse checked on me once after she gave me the news and then went back to her station. I was alone. My father was working. My mother was taking care of Terri. Ted's mother had no transportation to the hospital. There was no one.

I had never felt so frightened, so abandoned, so all alone. I clutched the rosary in my pocket that I had instinctively grabbed off my dresser before I left the house. It was small comfort, but was my only lifeline in a sinking world.

My tears flowed uncontrollably. Suddenly, out of nowhere, I thought I heard singing. It was soft angelic music, like a heavenly choir. I must be imagining things, I thought to myself, but the music persisted. As I listened closely, I realized it was coming from behind a closed door in the waiting room.

I got up and moved to the door. The singing was louder and definitely coming from the other side. I slowly opened the door and walked out onto a small balcony overlooking the hospital chapel. Down below a group of nuns were chanting and singing their evening prayers with sweet, angelic voices. God used these sisters to reassure me of His presence. I was not alone. He had not abandoned me after all.

I sat on the balcony mesmerized by the hymns and prayers until I heard voices in the waiting room. It was my family. My brother canceled his plans for the evening and brought my mother and mother-in-law to the hospital. My two sisters also gave up their homecoming dates to baby-sit for Terri. God not only gave me His spiritual presence, but also the loving support of my family when I needed them the most.

The doctors removed as much of the gunshot as they could from Ted's chest and upper body. One BB had penetrated his left eye and two others lodged dangerously close to his right eye. Neither BB could be removed safely. We were told that until the swelling went down and the blood dissipated, the extent of visual damage could not be determined.

Within a few days, Ted's sight returned in his right eye. In his left, all he could see was light and dark around the periphery. We hoped and prayed for an entire year for a miracle to restore his vision in that eye, but it never happened. He eventually had to have the eye removed, but, by the grace of God, has functioned as any normal adult. All my fears of an altered lifestyle were unfounded. The accident never prevented Ted from doing anything he wanted to do, or from living a normal, active life. He was even able to reclaim his position as second baseman on the softball team.

Having vision in only one eye does present a challenge, however, especially in depth perception. Whenever Ted is tempted to feel sorry for himself, he fingers the two BBs still lodged in his right eye socket and knows that he did indeed receive a miracle, just not the one he had initially prayed for.

A Few Quick Antioxidant-Feel-Good Chocolate Fixes

Three Low Calorie Fixes

Rosemarie Gortler

Take three chocolate kisses and have each one melt in your mouth. Say a prayer between kisses.

Dip 5 banana slices in a little bit of melted chocolate as your prayer gives praise to God.

Fix a steaming cup of hot chocolate—diet or regular—as your scale dictates. Sip it while you thank God for past blessings.

THANK YOU, GOD—FOR CHOCOLATE !

Five Kids and a Dog

Rosemarie Gortler

*"For He will give His angels charge of you
to guard you in all your ways."
(Psalm 91:1)*

    Picture a grown woman dressed the way nurses used to dress—in a white uniform with white shoes and stockings—standing atop a huge mound of dirt at a new housing construction site, with hands cupped over her mouth, repeatedly calling, "Nemesis, Nemesis."

That was me! As I think back to that day I wonder how many people saw that picture, heard me shouting and decided I had lost my mind.

Then, picture a parked car below that mound of dirt with five teary kids looking up at their mother. Sounds strange—right? The workers at the construction site beyond that mound of dirt all stopped working on the house they were building to stare open-mouthed at this strange picture. You can bet they were questioning the woman's sanity.

The story has an explanation though. Let me explain. I'm really sane. Honest!

~~~

The story began with a new puppy that we named Nemesis. I won Nemesis—or Nemi—as we called him—with a 10-cent church-school raffle ticket. I had never won *anything* before, so when my daughter begged, "*Please-please- please* buy a ticket to win the Pastor's dog's six-week-old puppy," I acquiesced. Nemi was the product of a love affair between a Belgian Shepherd that sneaked into the Pastor's back yard to frolic with Pastor's purebred German shepherd. The disappointed Pastor had definite plans to breed his purebred dog the following week. Anyway, Nemi was born and at the time of the raffle she was six weeks old. A really cute pup. But I didn't want a pup—cute or not. I had five elementary school children and a much needed job to help pay for necessary orthodontia and orthopedic work.

So, there I was, standing on that mound of dirt in my snow-white uniform because within a couple of months that cute puppy captured not only the kids' hearts, but Dad's and Mom's hearts, too. Nemi had run off with several dogs that morning. She was nowhere in sight and being so young, her return seemed impossible.

~~~

A couple of months before that bizarre morning on the mound, I was climbing into bed when the phone rang. The caller, my cousin Marianne, was laughing so hard that it took time for me to comprehend that Marianne was at the church raffle and we had just won the Pastor's pup.

I shouted into the phone in a loud screech, "No-what will I do with a dog?" My voice was so loud that I woke up the kids and they all came running to my room.

They whooped and hollered, dancing up and down—thrilled at the prospect of having a puppy. I was completely numb, "What will I do with a puppy?" I mumbled something about my plate being more than full. I kept mumbling about working three days a week, volunteering at the kids' school, keeping house and having no time left for a dog. Holding my hands on the side of my head I kept talking about Dad's around the clock shift work and his travel time that kept him away for twelve hours a day. I mumbled and they hopped around excitedly. They weren't listening—too busy planning for their new canine family member.

They knew Mom and Dad wouldn't refuse the dog. Especially since I started praying aloud for help with taking on a new puppy chore. Now I was talking to myself out loud, "This pup will be my nemesis." Our second oldest, Marigrace, was 10 years old at that time and the word "nemesis" had a nice sound to her, despite not knowing what it meant. She continued to jump up and down again, clapping her hands and said, "That's a good name, we'll call her Nemesis—Nemi for short." The other kids agreed. Maybe they thought it would please me. I was too numb to answer.

So Nemesis became a family member for the almost eighteen years of her life.

~~~

Back to my story.

Nemi was not even six months old when she left our back yard early that morning to run with several other dogs that appeared from nowhere. The kids were devastated when they realized that their dog had run away. Someone hadn't closed the gate.

I had to get to work and they had to get to school, but I did take some time to ride around and search for Nemi. That's what I was doing on that mound of dirt shouting Nemi's name. I never expected Nemi to come home—she was so young and she had run with bigger dogs.

I tried to gently prepare us for this probability. I wiped their tear stained faces and kissed each one as they slowly got out of the car and walked toward the school entrance. I was tearing too. Nemi had become so much a part of the family. Losing her would be hard to accept. I reminded them that they could pray very hard for their Guardian Angels to lead Nemi home. God would hear their prayers but Nemi had to cooperate. I promised to alert the neighbors and said I would put an ad in the lost and found newspaper column. They were sad—I was sad and we all agreed to pray—hard.

Our prayers were swiftly answered. When I returned home Nemi was in the back yard romping with the kids. It was a heartwarming scene that I have never forgotten.

My Aunt Rose, our after school sitter, greeted me at the door with a big grin on her face. "Isn't it great," she beamed, "thank God Nemi came home. Those kids must have prayed really hard. She came back alone and looked scared until the kids were here. She looks happy now."

From that day on, everyone remembered to close the back yard gate. We later noticed that Nemi didn't attempt to go near or out the gate. That day must have been a harrowing experience for her, too.

But—how in Heaven's name did that pup find her way home?

I believe I do know how she found her way home. God heard every one of our prayers and sent five or maybe six, counting mine—guardian angels to lead our Nemi away from the other dogs and back to us!

Thank you, Lord—and the Angels, too!!!

Prayer, Faith and a Bit of Chocolate

A Mother's Undying Love

Diane Carroll Vogel

"For everything there is a season... A time to be born, and a time to die; .... A time to weep, and a time to laugh; a time to mourn, and a time to dance...."
(Ecclesiastes 3:1-2,4)

    Mom smiles at me from picture frames and photo albums. Her green cardigan sweater, brittle with age, hangs in my closet. Her letters fill a keepsake box. Mom died at the age of 76 on December 6, 1988, but a few days later, I received a surprise gift, one I will forever associate with her.
    The holiday season was well under way when my husband, Tom, and I returned from my mother's funeral in Michigan to our home in Virginia. Obviously, I was not in a holiday mood, but I told Tom we should still attend his Rotary Club's annual Christmas party that week. For his sake, I would try to put on a cheerful front.
    When the party's organizer announced he was going to select someone from each table to talk about a special Christmas present, however, anxiety set in. I just knew he was going to pick me, and he did. Tears filled my eyes as I headed for the front of the room. I wanted to tell everyone about a unique gift from my mother, but staying composed was going to be difficult.
    The first part of my story took place when I was 6 years old. Two of the presents Santa Claus left me were especially wonderful, a baby doll and a small trunk. Inside the trunk were several doll outfits, including a white, dotted-swiss sundress with a matching pinafore apron, an ivory gown trimmed in white lace,

a pale violet dress with a matching bonnet and a yellow flannel nightgown with blue flowers. I was thrilled!

Although I treasured Baby Doll for years, by the time I was 7, I started doubting the existence of a jolly fat man in a red suit who slid down chimneys with a bag full of toys. That's when my parents showed me a ragged scrap of red fabric. A piece of Santa's suit must have caught on a brick in the chimney, they told me. My mother was a wonderful weaver of fanciful stories and my father a willing accomplice. I think they prolonged the Christmas myth about the jolly old elf partly for my benefit, and partly because they enjoyed playing Santa.

Mom's being a whopper of a storyteller drew chuckles from my audience, which included many parents and grandparents. Sharing this episode about Santa and his pants lifted my spirits as well. However, I told them this was not my favorite part of the Baby Doll story.

Years after I discovered Mom and Dad were the real Mr. and Mrs. Claus, my mother finally revealed she was the one who made Baby Doll's wardrobe. I wish she had told me earlier. Her gift was even more meaningful because she made it herself.

I have imagined the romanticized scene many times in my mind. After my two sisters and I were asleep, Mom would slip down to the basement with an armful of dress patterns, pieces of fabric and bits of lace and ribbon. Humming Christmas carols, she would bend over her treadle-operated, Singer sewing machine and construct little outfits for the doll she had hidden away.

Afterward, she would add small snaps and buttons and fancy frills to each garment painstakingly by hand. Night after night, she would work contentedly in secret on this special Santa present for her youngest daughter.

Most mothers from my generation were adept at mending and darning, but mine had never taken sewing lessons and was not an experienced seamstress. That's why her gift was so endearing. "Boy, Mom," I remember saying, "Those tiny stitches and trim must have been hard for you." She simply smiled and said, "They were." Pride and pleasure shone in her eyes.

Although Baby Doll is long gone, the remainder of her wardrobe is tucked away in pink tissue. Most of the dresses are frayed and have clumsily patched seams, which were mended by me when I was a little girl. In my memories, though, the clothes and the dressmaker remain beautiful.

I paused for a moment before concluding my Christmas story. Although I would always cherish my mother's handcrafted gift, talking about it to the Rotary Club members and their guests was painful as well as cathartic. After taking a deep breath, I told them my mother's funeral had taken place only a few days before and my story was a tribute to her.

As I looked about the silent room, I could see empathy reflected in my listeners' eyes. Some people were crying. This was supposed to be a festive party, and I wanted to end my narrative on an upbeat note. "When you get together with your families over the holidays," I said with a smile, "give each one of them a big hug. Showing affection openly and often is one of the greatest gifts we can give those we love."

When I finished speaking, the activity director handed me a "just for fun" recycled present, one of several he had collected from around his house. Each of the evening's storytellers received one. When I realized mine was a souvenir spoon from Canada, I was astonished.

On the handle of the small silver spoon were a red maple leaf and five stars. My mother was born in Canada, and my parents, sisters and I made a family of five. My eyes brimmed with tears. Most people would consider the spoon a charming coincidence, but a coincidence nonetheless.

For me, the spoon from Canada was much more. I believed Mom wanted her grieving daughter to receive a final Christmas gift to remember her by, and had a heavenly hand in directing one my way.

Death does not separate us from those we love. They come to us through dreams, old letters, mementos, and cherished memories—such as Santa, a seamstress and a silver spoon.

The Holy Spirit Even Helps With Housework

Rosemarie Gortler

"Pray in the Spirit at all times in every prayer and supplication." (Ephesians 6:18)

What a week!

Uncle Charlie died last Saturday. On Monday morning I was told that I needed two biopsies. On Monday afternoon our daughter called to say she was immediately leaving her home in Florida to be with Claire, our granddaughter, in Georgia.

Claire had been hospitalized with a ruptured appendix and was scheduled for surgery the next morning.

That's a week I had to give to the Lord—it was too much for me.

My husband, Fred, and his brother had planned to meet in Florida on Wednesday to prepare Uncle Charlie's funeral, but because our daughter sounded so frightened, I suggested that he leave right away and drive to Georgia to be with them. Following Claire's surgery, when her condition was stable, he could go on to Florida as planned. He agreed—our daughter and granddaughter needed support.

I had to stay in town because I had two oncology appointments on Wednesday. Those appointments are hard to get and rescheduling requires an act of Congress. My husband insisted I stay home to keep those appointments. It wasn't what I wanted to do, but I knew it was what I had to do. I would be in frequent contact by phone and I could pray for Uncle Charlie and Claire.

The next day was Tuesday, 6-6-06, and the early morning TV news was full of dire predictions about whether "the evil one" was in charge for the day. Getting out of bed, I shuffled to the kitchen for coffee. Chuckling, I loudly announced to the world, "God's always in charge, silly." I apologized to God for silly TV superstitions.

Pouring a cup of coffee, I opened the refrigerator door for milk. Wham! The shelf on the door came apart, spilling the contents of milk, juice and other bottles all over the floor. What a mess!

Looking again, I noticed that the roast I had defrosted yesterday was "bleeding" all over the refrigerator. I had planned to cook it for dinner last night, but after hearing about Claire, it was forgotten. Yuk! I felt overwhelmed and I wanted to cry. Pulling myself together, I took a deep breath and wondered, "Was this a 6-6-06 joke? Nah! Sorry, Lord, I'm being silly, too.

I need You now. You know how anxious I am these days—about everything. Forgive me—please."

The entire refrigerator shelf and both bottom drawers were a gooey, bloody mess. I still wanted to cry, but I pulled myself together again and talked to the Holy Spirit while I prepared the roast and put it in the microwave. I didn't want to be bothered with fancy roast preparation or an oven. Just cook the darn thing and get it out of my way.

God helps us in petty circumstances as well as in great and important situations, so I prayed. "OK, Holy Spirit—You know how overwhelmed I am. I can't take much more. Fred and I usually work together to replace this old refrigerator door shelf and those drawers with all the parts. You know how hard it is to get this old thing together. I'm a stressed mess. Help me, please, Holy Spirit."

Fred comes close to using language we don't usually use every time I clean this dinosaur with the duct taped shelf. He helps to put it back together. It's a two-man job. I make threats about buying a new model, but after it's clean we forget the threats.

"Holy Spirit, Fred is on two missions of Mercy and I need You to help me."

Still talking aloud, I proceeded to remove the shelf, drawers and the little snaps that hold things together. After cleaning the bloody mess, I used a disinfectant and once again called upon the Holy Spirit. "Let's go, Holy Spirit—I'll hold the shelf and You guide it in."

Amazing! The glass shelf slid right in—the first time in thirteen years—and the difficult to align drawers with all their parts fit together quickly and easily.

"Thank you, Holy Spirit—thank you—thank you—thank you!"

~~~

- 45 -

The microwave called out with the familiar "ding-ding" and I looked over and shook my head, noticing that I had forgotten to cover the roast. Now—I had a caked on microwave mess! But—surprisingly—it wiped up in a flash. All I had to do was wipe it quickly. The Holy Spirit is thorough.

You probably can't imagine how we always wrestled to clean that 'frig unless you have an old one like ours—with duct tape neatly holding the bottom shelf together. The duct tape worked—until that day. You might not believe the Holy Spirit helped me clean that day, but I am more than certain of His help.

How did the Spirit help? I don't know how God does anything.

Did He guide the parts in? Maybe He held my hand to do it. I only know that the shelf and those parts never before went in without giving us a real fight.

I also know—for sure—that God is present in our everyday lives in small things as well as in crises. I always receive His comfort. His answer is not always what I pray for, but He makes me know that He is here. This is the first time I asked for such a mundane request—cleaning help. And—I believe The Holy Spirit comforted me this way because of my other sorrows and also because I pleaded for His help.

Now, Holy Spirit—Uncle Charlie is in a better place and we will continue to pray for him. We are grateful that Claire is coming along—albeit very slowly—so how about helping me to cope with the upcoming biopsy reports and the cancer treatment that is sure to follow? I know I will need Your help—again.

~~~

Are you in a bind and overwhelmed? Feeling at wits end? Ask the Holy Spirit to help you cope with any situation. He'll comfort you, and help you, sometimes in very unexpected ways.

Mint Chocolate Brownies

Sallie Bachar

It's not always easy to follow in the footsteps of Jesus. Some days it requires great faith and a little extra work. But, like this recipe for mint chocolate brownies that has been in my family for years, it is well worth the effort! Chocolate brownies are also distracting!

Mint Chocolate Brownies

Brownies:
- 2 eggs
- 1 cup sugar
- ½ cup chopped nuts
- ½ cup flour
- 2 oz. unsweetened chocolate
- ½ cup butter or margarine, melted

Filling:
- 1 ½ cups powdered sugar
- 3 tablespoons butter or margarine, softened
- 2 tablespoons milk
- ¾ teaspoon peppermint extract
- few drops green food coloring

Glaze:
- 1/3 cup chocolate chips
- 2 tablespoons butter or margarine

Prepare brownies. Beat together eggs and sugar. Add nuts, flour, chocolate and melted butter. Stir until smooth. Spread in greased 8 inch square pan and bake at 350 degrees for 25 minutes. Cool.

Prepare filling. Cream together sugar, butter, milk and peppermint extract until smooth. Add food coloring and spread over brownies. Chill 1 hour.

Prepare glaze. Melt together chocolate chips and butter. Drizzle over filling and chill for 30 minutes before serving.

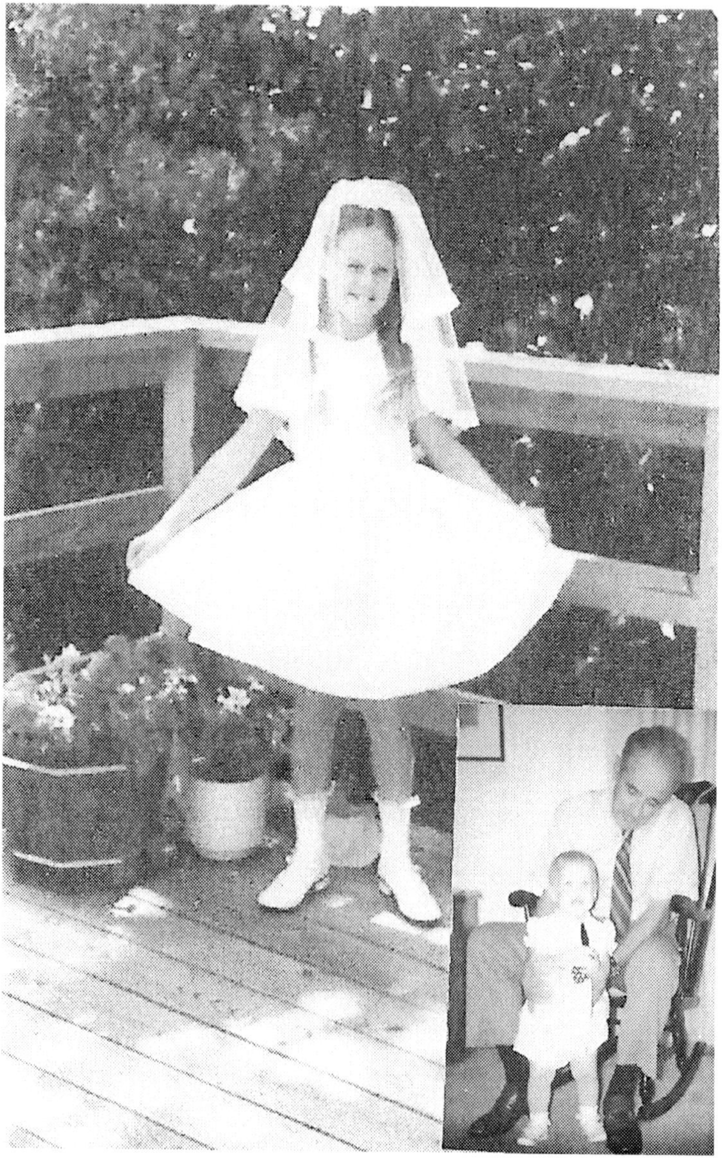

Thank You Lord

Diane Carroll Vogel

*"It is good to give thanks to the Lord,
to sing praise to Your Name, Most High,
To proclaim Your kindness at dawn
and Your faithfulness throughout the night...."*
(Psalm 92:1-3)

Anyone who has been the parent of a teenager knows the teen years can be traumatic at times. In November 1992, my daughter miraculously survived a near fatal accident. Memories of that event still haunt me, but Thanksgiving will forever have a special, spiritual meaning because of it.

Our seventeen-year-old daughter, Christine, was heading for a friend's house after work the evening before the holiday. Somehow, her attention was diverted. Perhaps she was fiddling with the radio or checking her makeup in the mirror. Perhaps she had taken a wrong turn at some point. Regardless, she did not realize a concrete barrier loomed just ahead on this dead-end street. By the time she saw the barrier, it was too late to avoid smashing into it.

The concrete cracked in half and the car was totaled, but amazingly, Christine escaped with minor injuries. People in a nearby house heard the crash and rushed to her aid. They called the police and us, and took Christine into their home until we arrived. The grandmother who lived with the family held her hand the entire time and prayed with her.

A policeman was already on the scene when my husband and I got there. We were frantic, but the officer was supportive and compassionate when he talked to us. He assured us our daughter was okay and said she was very fortunate. He even told us he had a similar accident when he was young. But one of his observations chilled us. He said the impact of the car hitting the cement barrier was so forceful, Christine should have been killed, or at least badly injured.

When I saw Christine walking toward us with one of her rescuer's arms around her shoulders, I breathed a sigh of relief. She really was okay. But Christine had something even more astonishing to tell us when we got back home.

For one thing, Christine was not wearing her seatbelt. She remembered bouncing up from her seat when the car struck the barrier head-on. Terrified because she knew a crash was inevitable, she whispered a prayer to her grandfather. Granddaddy died when she was five, but she always felt a strong attachment to him. She believed he was with her that terrible night and, by God's grace, saved her life.

Had Frank Vogel's spirit interacted on Christine's behalf? Had he saved her life?

Like many teenagers, my daughter was going through some tough times, but she still believed in the power of prayer. I was grateful to God for Christine's faith, and that He answered her prayer.

Christine, her father and I were also appreciative of the kindness shown by the couple who took care of Christine in her time of need. Our daughter said she felt especially comforted when the family's grandmother held her hand and prayed with her. Truly, these three people were God's ministering angels.

On Thanksgiving Day, our family was still distraught over Christine's horrifying ordeal, even while we celebrated her miraculous escape from harm. I remained shaken by the thought that Christine could have died, but my heart rejoiced over our own blessings and I gave thanks to God for protecting her.

My thoughts drifted back to the day my daughter made her First Communion. Her religious education teacher had given her a holy card. On it was a sweet picture of Jesus giving communion to a little girl. Christine added the following prayer to this card: "God, please watch me and my family. Every morning and every night watch us God please to keep us safe. But watch us in all sorts of ways."

I have always believed in miracles and the power of prayer. God's grace was with Christine during her near fatal accident, and He has watched over her in all sorts of ways throughout her thirty-two years. I believe He has a special plan for her, which He will reveal in time.

Prayer, Faith and a Bit of Chocolate

And He Sent His Angels

Rosemarie Gortler

"Pray without ceasing."
(1Thessalonians: 5:17)

Are angels active in our lives? You can bet on it! Paramedics miraculously found our son Rick's car on the side of busy Interstate 91, outside of New Haven Connecticut, and brought him to the St. Raphael Hospital emergency room. They reported that his pulse was down to 20 when they found him. The emergency room nurse later told us how "lucky" he was. She added that he had been "on his way out."

We know what lucky means—it means "blessed"—cared for by the angels we had been persistently praying God would send. Our prayer pleaded, "Please Lord, send your angels to protect Rick from harm when he has these passing out episodes." Rick had been passing out without warning for more than a year and the many physicians he saw could not give reason or prescribe treatment. Finally, following this episode his new physician, Dr. Mark Schoenfeld, diagnosed the problem and scheduled a pacemaker implant to be done the next day. He would finally receive the treatment he needed.

~~~

Rick had been experiencing these episodes for more than a year and all he heard from doctors was, "You have to learn to relax."

That was the essence of every doctor's diagnosis given to Rick, a hard working, active, enthusiastic and spiritual young man in his thirties. His fainting episodes occurred every once in a while without warning. It was frightening because he never—not even once—had a physical sign that he would lose consciousness. He would just fall down. He was still driving—with the doctors' OK and to his family's horror—but the doctors assured him that this only happened when he was tired.

On one occasion, he lost consciousness and fell from a forklift at work. He came home one evening and losing consciousness, fell over as he walked through the door. There were several other frightening episodes.

Meanwhile, his usual high energy level was rapidly falling. He was tired all the time. Following the implant he confessed to us that he used to become so fatigued that even taking a shower wore him down. He would have to rest after a shower in order to have the energy to drive to work.

As the Regional Manager of a large hardware chain, he pushed himself to do his work. He was clearly in physical crisis but wouldn't admit it to himself and didn't want to worry his family. But we could tell there was something very wrong.

We prayed hard for an accurate diagnosis and medical wisdom for treatment. We kept asking God to send angels to watch over him at all times.

We wondered if God was listening to our prayers when Rick was promoted to Regional Manager and transferred from Virginia to Connecticut. "Please God, hear our prayers—Rick is a caring husband and father and loves You so much—heal him—please—send your angels to keep him from danger."

As usual, God knew the better way to go. While driving to work one morning, Rick had a premonition—an aura. He knew he had to pull over, call 911 and tell them to send an ambulance to exit 10 of Interstate 91. That was the **only** warning he had ever received! And—there are **three** #10 exits on I-91. He never indicated which exit!

The angels certainly did watch over Rick. The ambulance arrived within minutes and he was whisked to the St. Raphael

Hospital emergency room where he was diagnosed and treatment began.

Thank you Lord, for hearing our prayers and sending Rick to a place he could be treated and to a fine cardiologist who knew exactly what to do.

Following the pacemaker* implant surgery, Dr. Schonfeld from the Connecticut St. Raphael Hospital assured my daughter-in-law and our family that Rick, "would be just fine." We were assured that Rick's scary "passing out" episodes that had been occurring intermittently for over a year would end. The pacemaker would be "curative."

That was several years ago and Rick is once again the fun-loving, active, involved father he was before all this began. He is also very grateful to God for sending those angels to watch over him—as we all are.

We did a mighty lot of praying during that time. Specifically, my prayer was that God would send angels to watch over him—and He did.

A pacemaker is an electronic device used to treat patients who have abnormally slow heartbeats. The device generates signals to the heart when necessary, causing it to beat faster, thus maintaining normal heartbeats. This normal heart rate ensures that enough oxygen and nutrients are delivered through the blood to all organs of the body.

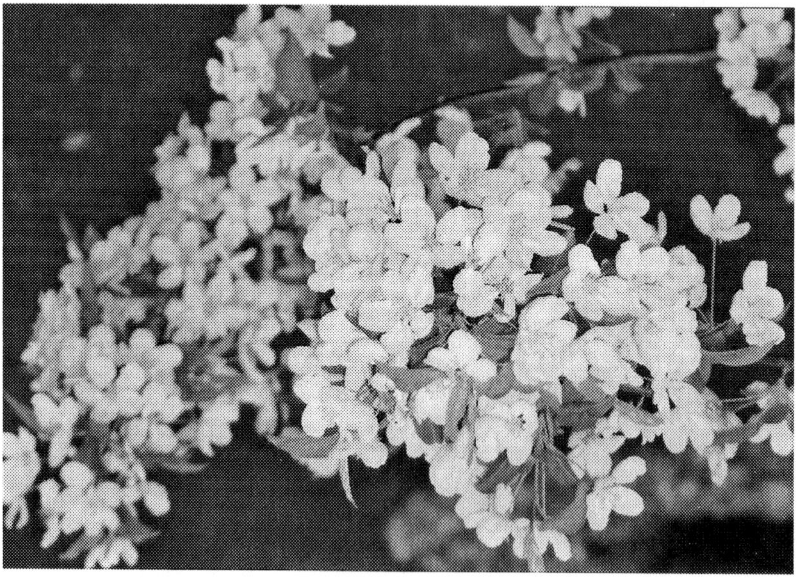

Apple Blossoms in September

Sallie Bachar

"Great indeed, we confess, is the mystery of our religion."
(1Timothy 3:16)

The emotional roller coaster I had been riding for the last several days was wearing me out. I needed a break, a few hours of rest. I left my husband, Ted, alone at the hospital and came home to try to get some sleep. We had been spending the last four days and nights at the bedside of my dying mother-in-law.

Mom amazed the hospital staff with her tenacious hold on life. Each morning they told us she would probably not make it through the day, and each evening they told us she would probably not make it through the night. It hurt to see her suffer so much. But God had His own timing, and He wasn't ready to call her home just yet.

I was chilled to the bone when I got home and changed into warm sweatpants and a comfortable sweatshirt. Exhausted but unable to sleep, I stared mindlessly out my bedroom window at the rain pounding against the glass.

- - - - - -

The last time I saw the sun was Wednesday, the day we admitted Mom into the hospital. As Ted helped put his mother on the stretcher and into the medical van, she asked him to stop for a few moments so she could look up at the blue, cloudless, September sky for one last time. In a hushed voice, she whispered, "It's so beautiful!"

- - - - - -

The wind blew hard, whipping through the little apple tree Ted had planted two years ago beneath the bedroom window. Flowering crab trees are my special herald of spring with their tiny, pink, fragrant blossoms. They are a welcome sight after a long Wisconsin winter, and he purposely planted the tree right under the window so I could enjoy its beauty every morning upon rising.

I was praying that the tender branches wouldn't break in the strong wind when I caught sight of something strange and unnatural for this time of year. Little pink buds had appeared on the very topmost branches. For some inexplicable reason, the tree had started to blossom again.

In northern Wisconsin, crab apple trees flower for only a short time. Depending upon the weather, they only bloom in mid May for about two weeks. Then the fragile petals fall one by one, coaxed off by the slightest whisper of a breeze. Not only was this second blooming unusual for September, but it was also puzzling that successive days of cold, rainy weather couldn't shake the flowers off.

I have no idea if other trees in the area were also blossoming, but as I pondered this strange phenomenon, I felt this was God's special, comforting gift to soothe my aching heart. Although Mom's earthly existence was passing away, He seemed to be telling me that she would soon blossom in His eternal springtime.

My thoughts wandered back again to Mom in the hospital. How fragile and small she seemed as the cancer ravaged through her body, and yet she was clinging tenaciously to life, her heart beating strong and defying all the doctors' predictions.

She was diagnosed with colon cancer two years ago at the age of eighty. She refused chemotherapy after only one treatment because of its side effects and instead, chose to live out her remaining days feeling as good as she could for as long as she possibly could. A woman of deep faith, she wasn't afraid to die. She spoke openly of her death and was grateful for the long life she had lived.

She remained at home until my stepfather-in-law could no

longer care for her, and made the decision herself to enter the hospital, fully knowing this was the end. We called Ted's brother to come as soon as possible, and all three of our children, who were very close to Grandma, made arrangements to come home for the weekend also to say goodbye. We all expected a funeral on Monday, but Mom wasn't ready for that yet.

She remained awake and alert until the last grandchild arrived late Friday night. Although it was difficult for her to talk, she made the effort to speak to each one individually. All her life she put her family first before herself, and she wasn't any different as she lay dying. She still admonished her sons— one to quit smoking and the other one to relax and slow down. She said goodbye to each one of her grandchildren and left them words to carry in their hearts.

I was the only one she didn't speak to in those final hours, but she had done all her talking to me over the last six months when the cancer began to take its toll. Mom loved me and treated me as the daughter she never had from the moment I first dated her son. She was my friend, as well as my mother-in-law, and when my own mother died suddenly when I was twenty-seven, she stepped in and filled the void in my life. She shared her faith, her strength, her encouragement, and her love with me. Words were unnecessary between us.

The whole family gathered around her bedside, and only after her private conversations with each one, did she start to slip in and out of consciousness. She whispered of seeing her brother, her first husband, and other family members that had died and told us how happy they were, and then she surprised us all when she said in a strong voice, "Don't you cry for me!"

When Sunday afternoon arrived, Mom's heart was still beating as strong as ever. The family couldn't stay indefinitely, and one by one they returned to their own homes and college, leaving me and Ted alone to keep vigil with her. It was after they all left and I was home by myself that I discovered the apple blossoms.

For the next two days, I got up early and checked on Mom before I went to work. I came again after work and stayed at her bedside until 8 p.m. when Ted relieved me. He remained with her until two or three in the morning and then came home for a few hours sleep before starting his day.

Before I went to the hospital, however, I looked out the window to see if the apple blossoms were still there. I felt that when the blossoms were gone she would be, too. By Tuesday, most of them had been battered off by the wind and rain leaving only a few still clinging stubbornly to life.

Early Wednesday morning, a strange feeling overtook me. I sensed this was not the day to go to work and hurriedly dressed in jeans and a tee shirt and left within minutes for the hospital.

When I arrived, Mom's breathing was very shallow and erratic. I knew it wouldn't be long. I called Ted at home and told him to come right away. The rain had finally stopped after a week of intermittent showers and thunderstorms, but it was still cloudy and gloomy. How I longed for the sunshine and for Mom to be at peace.

The nurse entered the room a short time later. She put Vaseline on Mom's cracked and dried lips, making them shiny, and turned her head to face the window. Her breathing became slower and slower with long pauses between breaths. The end was very near.

Just then the clouds opened up and the sun shone through the window directly on Mom's face, casting an angel-like glow upon her. One last breath, and she slipped away ever so peacefully. A faint smile was left on her softened lips just before the gray clouds swallowed the sun once again.

In my haste to get to the hospital, I had forgotten to look at the apple tree before I left the house early that morning, but there was no need to look now. I knew the last blossom was gone.

Ann's Chocolate Trifle
Diane Carroll Vogel

We worry. We pray. And sometimes we turn to chocolaty comfort food as a pleasant if temporary form of stress release. Note that *stressed* spelled backwards is *desserts*. My mother-in-law's palate pleasing trifle is sure to *de-stress* the chocolate cravers in your family.

Ingredients

1 small box of dark chocolate cake mix (or store bought, chocolate pound cake)
1 4-serving size box of chocolate fudge pudding mix (not instant)
8-ounce container of creamy whipped topping
miniature size chocolate bits
trifle dish or deep, glass bowl

Directions

1. Bake the cake according to directions on the box. Cut the cooled cake into bite size pieces.
2. Cook the pudding according to directions on the box, but decrease the milk to 1 1/3 cups. Let the pudding cool.
3. Layer the bottom of the trifle dish with 1/3 each of cake, pudding and whipped topping. Sprinkle chocolate bits on the top.
4. Continue to add layers until all the ingredients are gone. Refrigerate this dessert for at least three hours before serving.

Thank you, Lord, for the simple indulgences you allow us in our daily lives.

Surviving Stress with Smiles, Hugs, Laughter and Chocolate

Stress can raise blood pressure, cause us to hyperventilate, make muscles tight and painful, bring on headaches and a myriad of other "pains in the neck" or "pains elsewhere."

De-Stress by following the advice of some experts:

- Lucy of the *Peanuts* comic strip by Charles Schultz advises, "All I really need is love, but a little bit of chocolate now and then doesn't hurt."
- Virginia Satir, noted author and psychotherapist recommends, "We need 4 hugs a day for survival. We need 8 hugs a day for maintenance. We need 12 hugs a day for growth." *May we add that you can ask for hugs and also hug yourself. It feels good.*
- Bill Keane of *Family Circus* tells us, "A hug is like a boomerang – you get it back right away."
- Mother Theresa told us, "Peace begins with a smile." She also noted that "Every time you smile at someone, it is an action of love, a gift to that person, a wonderful thing."

And your humble authors add ways to laugh:

- Alone, or with a friend, chant "Ha Ha Ha Ho" until the belly laughs begin.
- Make funny faces in a mirror or with children until laughter reigns.
- Rent a funny movie, watch funny TV, read jokes and share them at the dinner table.
- Tell stories about funny things that happened to you.

The American Academy of Cardiology recommends 15 minutes of good laughing daily to reduce the effects of bad stress.

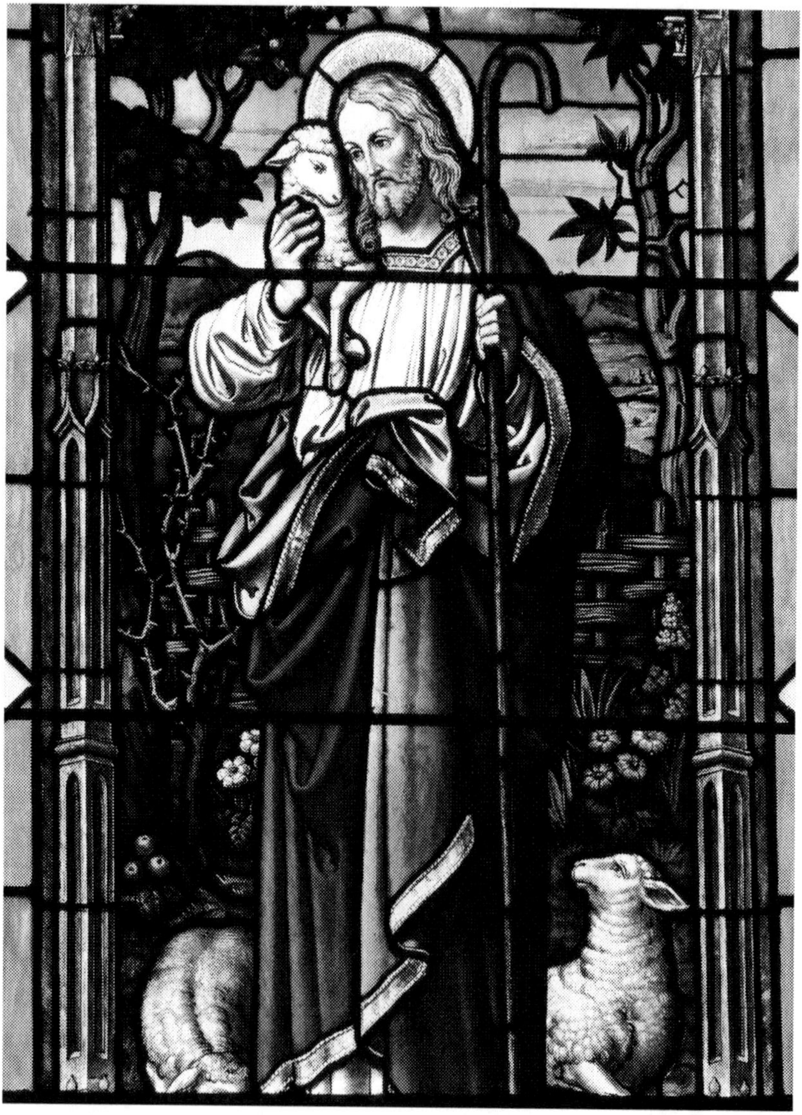

And Nicholas Lived

Rosemarie Gortler
As told by Renee Conell

*"I will praise You, Lord, with all my heart;
I will declare all Your wondrous deeds."
(Psalm 9:2)*

"Mrs. Conell, Nicholas has necrotizing fasciitis—in lay language, that's flesh eating bacteria." The orthopedic surgeon was speaking clearly but his words sounded repetitive and far away—like an echo. Another specialist, an infectious disease doctor, was hanging an intravenous bag into a central line which was inserted into Nick's arm. My knees buckled when he said, "If Nick is not taken to surgery immediately, he could lose his leg at the knee, at the hip—or be dead by morning."

My body went cold and my mind could hardly understand. The part about death reverberated until I wanted to scream and say, "No, you're wrong!"

How could this be? Just a few hours ago we came to see the doctor about what we thought was a high school wrestling injury.

Nick was speaking. He was talking about not being able to play football, lacrosse or wrestle with one leg. The whole scene was surreal.

The doctors continued discussing surgery and addressing me at the same time. They pulled the covers back to show me the infectious spread. It was horrifying to see that the thin red infection line on Nick's ankle that I had seen hours ago had already spread up Nick's leg and was pooling in the groin. My every thought began with a plea for God to heal our son.

The nightmare continued. I prayed and trusted that Nick was not going to die! I was going to take him home with or without a leg. I wasn't going to bury my son!

The surgeon was talking about doing an MRI prior to surgery to determine his course of surgical action. I continued to pray.

Nick went for the MRI and I hurried to call my friends to ask them to pray as hard as they could. They promised me they would call the priest to come to pray with Nick and to administer the Sacrament of the sick. My next call was to Larry, my husband. He was out of town. I really needed him to come home. He could be home early tomorrow morning. Relieved by this, I rushed to get back to Nick.

Back in the room, I hugged my son and grabbed his shoulders. "Nick, I'm taking you home with one leg or two legs, but you **are** coming home." I went on, "Nick, I need you to pray and to be strong." He smiled and nodded.

At this point the surgical decision was for 12 hours of antibiotic therapy to hopefully localize the infection prior to surgical intervention in the morning.

The surgeon stayed with us until 2:00 A.M. Nick was resting so I left to check on my daughter, to get myself together and I promised to return at 7:00 A.M.

~~~

The pastor was leaving Nick's room as I arrived a bit before 7:00. Pastor confided to my friend that Nick told him that he was certain that he was going to live. He had been praying all night and knew that his prayers were answered. Nick told the pastor that he had been feeling God's presence in the room all night. He said he heard God's voice within himself. Pastor smiled as he shared with my friend that Nick was a very special young man and that he was sure that God had something special in store for him. I found out about the pastor's visit later that week.

Nick had surgery the day before Thanksgiving and the day after as well. His scar starts at the ankle and goes right up to the knee. The incision was left open and packed for two days. The pain was excruciating. Nick didn't use the morphine pump as often as was allowed. Instead, he preferred to pray and give thanks. Both doctors were amazed at the progress. I was amazed and so very grateful for God's goodness and for the competency and dedication of both physicians.

Nick certainly did walk out of the hospital—albeit on crutches. He was changed by all of this. Three years after high school, Nick went off to South Africa for a year to teach in a school that his former high school supports. He touched lives and the young people he taught touched him—and some still stay in contact.

I agreed with our Pastor. God needed Nick to do His work on Earth—to be a pair of God's hands to serve others.

~~~

The family has changed along with Nick. The last six months prior to his illness had been full of necessary but unwanted family changes—moving to a new town, loss of daily contact with good friends and family and having to change occupations. We had begun to lose the way we related to each other. We were focusing on the past. This new gratitude we felt reminded us of all we have as a family. It was a wonderful new beginning, prompting us to focus on where we were going rather than where we had been.

Prayer, Faith and a Bit of Chocolate

The Good Samaritan

Diane Carroll Vogel

*"You shall love the Lord your God with all your heart,
with all your strength, and with all your mind;
and your neighbor as yourself."*
(Luke 10:25-27)

On the evening before Mother's Day, I headed for the mall to buy a new outfit. An upbeat tune was playing on the radio, and I bobbed my head in accompaniment. Then, within a ten-minute period, I narrowly avoided two collisions. "Crazy drivers," I thought. After parking my car and entering the mall, I was still frazzled. Maybe that's why I lost my checkbook.

I didn't discover the loss right away. Racks of colorful clothes beckoned, and I was a woman with a mission. Spurred on by my goal to find the perfect outfit, I banished my gloomy mood.

Unfortunately, when I went to pay for my selections two hours later, my checkbook was missing. I did not panic *yet*. After paying by credit card, I rushed to the parking lot. Surely the checkbook would be on the seat or floor of the car. Not so.

If it wasn't in the car, I reasoned, it must be at home. I called my husband. He searched the house while I waited nervously, cell phone to ear. When he was unable to locate the checkbook, we both became alarmed. I raced back to the store and retraced my steps before going to the lost and found department. Still no luck.

Finally, I hurried home—remembering to drive safely and watch out for bad drivers, of course. I did not want to double my troubles. By the time I got home, my stomach was in knots.

My husband, worried about what would happen if the checkbook fell into the wrong hands, greeted me with angry words. His rebukes made me feel even more stupid and careless. I made another desperate hunt for the checkbook, including rummaging through wastebaskets and laundry hampers. The only thing this futile search produced was a torrent of tears. Now panic set in.

Someone had access to the money in our account! Someone had our personal information. And, that same person had probably forged one of our signatures on a large check already. I felt sicker by the moment, but continued to search, pace and pray.

Meanwhile, my husband, the Financial Guy in our family, started taking preventative measures to secure our account. By now, he was more in control of his emotions, but I had almost abandoned hope. It was 11:00 P.M. Desperate, I bowed my head and asked Jesus to please help me.

Suddenly the phone rang and I grabbed for it. The caller, a stranger who identified herself as Linda, said she had found my checkbook. She knew I must be frantic and wanted to return my checkbook as soon as possible. She told me she had just returned home from the mall and called as soon as she located my number in the phonebook.

"Thank you, God," I whispered silently while Linda talked. Her soft-spoken voice was gentle and reassuring. I grew calmer. I was still crying, but now from relief. I thanked Linda profusely, and asked her if I could get my checkbook back right away even though it was late. When she agreed, I ran excitedly to share this good news with my husband.

As we drove the short distance to Linda's house, I reviewed my trip to the store. Amazingly, although I had entered the shopping center around 6:15 P.M., Linda had not spotted my checkbook in the mall hallway until around 9:40!

How it managed to work its way out of my purse, I'll never

know for sure. Why no one picked it up off the floor during those four hours, I will never understand. But how blessed I was that this kind and honest woman was the one who saw it and chose to locate the owner.

When we reached Linda's home, she was waiting for me, checkbook in hand. She would accept no reward, and after a short exchange of comments, simply asked, "Is everything all right now?" Indeed it was. I returned home lighthearted, relieved and wiser. From now on, I would double-check to make sure my purse was securely fastened. And, I would keep Linda on my Prayer List forever.

A miracle is an event involving divine intervention, or an amazing or wondrous event. The return of my checkbook wasn't dramatic or sensational, but it demonstrated both the power of prayer and the basic goodness of most people. Every day, numerous Good Samaritans show compassion for others without seeking praise or payment. To me, these are wondrous events indeed.

Faith instructs us to love our neighbors. Please, Lord, reward my earthly angel, Linda, for her honesty and sensitivity. And please, Lord, open my eyes and heart to those around me who are in need of my prayers and help.

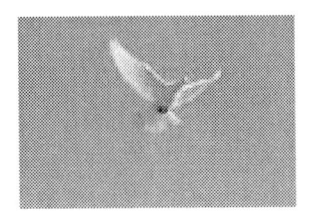

Prayer, Faith and a Bit of Chocolate

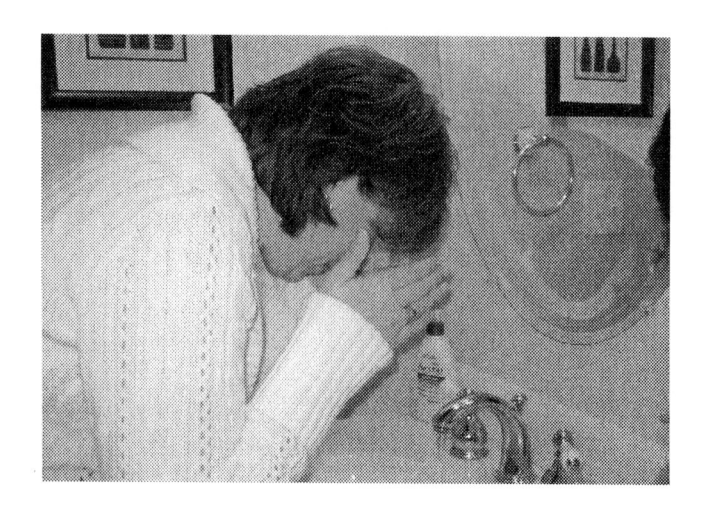

The Mascara Sign

Rosemarie Gortler
As told by Francine Gallagher

*"For Thou, O Lord, hast made me glad by Thy work;
at the works of Thy hands I sing for joy."*
(Psalm 92 1-4)

In my twenties, divorced, cynical and trying hard to support two young sons by working two—sometimes three jobs was tough going. I decided that earning a graduate degree was the best solution for supporting the three of us with one job.

Sure—parents, family and friends are supportive, but that's not the same as being a self supportive parent. I wanted to forget that people warned me about that marriage. Divorce is devastating. You feel like an abysmal failure, worry about the future and end up with a whopping case of low self image.

Helping me to cope with the anger at myself and my failure was the excuse that all men are the same and the world is at fault. So, I went about my business with the smile that's expected, sore feet and an aching back from long hours of waiting tables.

After work, I went home to the most important people in my life, my two great kids. I tried to be both a mom and a dad. I found snippets of time to take them rowing at the nearby lake and to other activities that a dad might do.

I remember taking my first final exam as a single mom. The babysitter cancelled at the last minute so I had to postpone taking it. On the rescheduled date, she cancelled again and I toted the baby to school thinking, "I can't chance losing this scholarship."

I longed to have someone there to hold my son for just a

few minutes. Feeding a baby by holding a bottle in your aching left arm and writing with your right hand makes for a sloppy exam paper. Sometimes it's hard to hold tears back but it has to be done. *Put up a good front. Get on with it.* But—pretending everything is fine is jet fuel for cynicism.

Life did get a bit easier with each year that went by. Just before my younger son entered kindergarten and my older son was going into second grade, my parents offered to share their late August vacation week in the Pocono Mountains. I gladly accepted.

We traveled in two cars because kindergarten registration was scheduled mid- vacation, necessitating my earlier return. My older son would stay on with his grandparents. Meanwhile, we would enjoy the journey by stopping at favorite places. I was more than ready to relax for a few days.

We stopped at Mount St. Mary's in Emmitsburg, Maryland, a favorite stop for my parents to pray at a replica of the Lourdes Grotto. A huge gold colored statue of Mary overlooks the Grotto area. My parents admired the statue, but my words projected my ever-present anger. "She looks *#*"—a vulgar term referring to my opinion of the expression on Mary's face.

Mom instantly shot back a reprimand declaring the comment disrespectful. Through narrowed eyes and in a low voice she asked how I expected my children to be respectful of me, of authority and of God with that kind of example. It was on the tip of my tongue to verbally shoot back a defense, but the shocked look on both parents' faces stopped me cold. The exchange ended as quickly as it began.

We proceeded down the path to the tiny chapel, stopping for a while at each of the stations along the way. I had to admit it was a peaceful place despite my change in attitude towards religion and religious places since my divorce.

The chapel doors stood open. We walked in. I planned to kneel at the rail to say a prayer, but a force pushed me down.

Surprised, I began a prayer—but a loud, clear voice within me interrupted with, "Jesus is displeased with you." A flood of tears followed—but I wasn't sad. I felt joy, not sadness. The tears continued to fill my eyes and roll down my cheeks.

Was I losing my mind? Confused and a little anxious, I asked for a sign that what was happening was real.

It occurred to me that my inexpensive mascara must have been running under my sunglasses. The funny thing was, I wasn't unhappy. I wanted to stay there—kneeling at the rail in prayer. I don't know how long I was there.

My parents and the kids left. My older son came back a while later and asked, "Mommy, when are you coming out?" I smiled at him and said," I'll be out in a minute." He went outside, satisfied with my response.

I don't know how much longer I remained kneeling. I do know I wanted to stay in God's peace—but I knew that this peace would stay with me—so I stood up, glad that my sunglasses provided protection not only from the sun but from the "raccoon" eyes caused by tears wet by cheap mascara.

I left the chapel. The family was completing the Rosary. I sat on a bench overlooking a pond and reflected on what happened in that small chapel. This wonderful peace was new to me. I wondered, "Was this feeling the sign I asked for?"

Everyone had begun walking quietly back to our vehicles. I asked Mom if she would ride with me and have the boys ride with Dad. She agreed adding, "Dad said he wanted to take them because the boys like riding in his truck."

I shared my chapel experience with Mom and took off my sunglasses to show her my raccoon eyes. She looked at me closely and said, "Your mascara isn't running, your face is clean." I quickly glanced at myself in the rear view mirror.

Incredible! I buy inexpensive makeup that runs with a hint of water. How could tears have been flowing so freely and...no running? *I asked for a sign that what I heard and felt was really happening—that I wasn't going crazy.*

We drove in relative silence for the remainder of the trip. I couldn't wait to park the cars, check into the motel and get to the room. Mom opened the door and I pushed past her to get to the sink to splash my face with water. *Sure enough, the mascara ran freely—down my cheeks.*

But the best and surest sign remained inside, my change of heart. The anger seemed to disappear. Joy and peace filled my heart—my smile was real.

Life didn't get too much easier, but not having so much anger and cynicism made it a lot easier to cope.

My annulment came through and seven years later I found and married a wonderful man. I've returned to the Grotto many times since that day.

Emergency Relief for Chocolate Cravings

Diane Carroll Vogel

- Try a dark chocolate kiss. Add a sweet kiss for your spouse. It's heart healthy!
- Escape to the bliss of a childhood memory as you munch on a chocolate candy bar from the good old days.
- Make s'mores. Place a piece of chocolate and a marshmallow on top of a graham cracker and microwave on a paper plate or paper towel for one minute. Share s'mores with your family and watch the smiles multiply.
- Keep a bag of miniature, chocolate candy bars in the freezer. Treat yourself to one or two when you are feeling blue.

Spontaneous prayers are the best pick-me-ups. They can be said anytime
and anywhere.
"Thank You, God, for Your many blessings."

Prayer, Faith and a Bit of Chocolate

A Belated Happy Birthday

Sallie Bachar

"A spiritual gift is given to each of us so we can help each other."

(1 Corinthians 12:7)

November 19, 1997. My fiftieth birthday—and one that I would never forget.

I wasn't dreading this milestone, but actually looking forward to it. The birth of my first grandchild could be any day. Maybe the baby would be born on my birthday. Sharing a birthday with my grandchild would be the blessing I hoped and prayed for. No party for me—just my son's phone call announcing that the baby was born.

Instead, I found myself in O'Hare International Airport. The phone call I received was not from Steve but from a doctor in the emergency room at a hospital in Toledo, Ohio. My youngest daughter, who was attending the university there, was admitted with a ruptured appendix.

Sandy had transferred from a small, private college in southern Wisconsin to the University of Toledo for her sophomore year. She tried to convince me and her father that it had one of the best programs for speech-language pathology, her major, but in truth, she was in love with her high school sweetheart and wanted to be closer to him. Andy, who was a year older than Sandy, was a member of the Coast Guard and was stationed on Lake Erie in Toledo. It was hard to let her go, but she was determined.

She had only been at school a little over two months when she called early one Sunday morning, in tears, and said she had a terrible pain in her stomach and didn't know what to do. Andy was in Virginia for three weeks at a training school. She was all alone and frightened.

I advised her to ask her roommate to take her to a walk-in clinic. I hung up the phone feeling so utterly helpless but confident that the clinic personnel would be able to help her. They called it indigestion and sent her back to the dorm with some medication.

The pain continued over the next three weeks. She visited the clinic again and also the campus health center. Nothing helped. Her symptoms were not typical of appendicitis, and being a college student, the doctors pointed to improper diet, stress, insufficient rest, or possibly an ulcer, as the cause of her pain.

I didn't know what to do. Each day I called hoping and praying she would tell me she was feeling better, but the pain got worse. In desperation she went once more to the campus health center. A different nurse was on duty and finally diagnosed her condition correctly. There was no time to waste. She was rushed to the hospital where surgery was performed immediately. It was seven p.m. and the only surgeon on call, by the grace of God, was the best on staff.

Andy was still away at training, and she was all alone. I had to go to her. It was too far to drive, and there were no more flights out that evening. I called a travel agent, who managed to get me a flight at eleven o'clock the next morning under an "emergency condition". I spent the rest of the night praying and begging God to keep her alive.

I had to go alone. My husband, Ted, is self-employed, and it was impossible for him to leave the business. Besides, money was tight. We couldn't afford two plane tickets. I didn't even know where the money would come from to cover the expenses of this trip. I only knew I had to go, and I trusted God to take care of everything else.

When morning came I was very anxious about flying—this was only my second time in an airplane. I remembered stories from my friends about O'Hare and the difficulties of connecting flights and finding your way around the huge terminal. I would laugh and tell them, "That's not for me!" My concern for Sandy, however, overcame all my fears, and somehow I managed to find my gate without any problems.

I had no hotel reservation, no rental car, and no idea where the hospital was or how I would get there once the plane landed. My only thought was for Sandy. The trip passed slowly. All the joy and anticipation of my fiftieth birthday and my soon-to-be-born grandchild vanished. Rain was falling outside the terminal windows, mingling with the tears falling from my eyes.

I arrived in Toledo twenty-four hours after the doctor's phone call from the previous night. A taxi took me to the hospital, a huge complex, and dropped me off at the entrance. Dragging my suitcase through the long halls, I finally found Sandy's room. The surgery was over, of course, by the time I arrived. The surgeon removed what was left of her appendix, but the rupture had spread poison throughout her body.

She looked so frail in that strange hospital bed, not like the bouncy, energetic college girl who left home two months ago. An IV dripped massive doses of antibiotics into her veins to combat the infection while other machines monitored her vital signs.

"She's a lucky young lady," said the surgeon. "If she had waited any longer, she might not be here."

Under normal circumstances, a patient would be dismissed in a day or two, but because of the seriousness of Sandy's condition, the doctor anticipated a week's stay. "She'll be home by Thanksgiving," he promised me.

A week? Thanksgiving? I was finally beginning to grasp the full impact of the situation. Where would I stay for a week? I couldn't afford a motel for that long nor the cab fare back and forth to the hospital. I wasn't even sure I had packed enough clothes.

Most patients, at that time, shared a room with another patient, but because no beds were available, the hospital put her in a private room at no additional cost. I could stay in her room and sleep in a chair. It wouldn't be the most comfortable but better than sharing a room with another patient and her visitors, I thought. Little did I know that God had taken care of me, too, and had made other arrangements.

The hospital had recently converted five classrooms into sleeping facilities in one of its adjacent buildings to rent in emergency situations to people like me. Someone had checked out just hours before my arrival. I could have the room, but for no more than five nights, at a cost of $25 per night. In addition, a shuttle between the buildings was available twenty-four hours a day, free of charge! I couldn't have asked for anything better.

I found the room very comfortable, spacious, and nicer than most motels I have stayed in. I retired late that night, exhausted, and still worried, but so very grateful. I slept only a few hours and then called the shuttle to take me to the hospital to spend the day with my daughter. She was still in a lot of pain but alert and happy to see me.

I had just sat down near her bed when the phone rang. It was early, only 7 A.M. It was the call I had waited for at home. "Hi, Grandma," said Steve. "Your new grandson tried so hard but just couldn't make it for your birthday." Colton Daniel was born at 5 A.M. on November 20th.

I didn't know how to react. Tears of joy and tears of sadness both trickled down my cheeks. I tried to grasp the irony of it all - one new life struggling to make his entry into the world while nine hundred miles away his new aunt struggled just to survive. And me, bridging the gap between the two – a new grandmother and still a mother whose heart suffered along with her own daughter.

Sandy made a remarkable recovery and was dismissed from the hospital four days later, on the very day that I needed to vacate the room God provided for my stay. We flew home together to celebrate a very special Thanksgiving and a belated happy birthday.

Prayer, Faith and a Bit of Chocolate

Mail Order Message

Sallie Bachar

"For we are God's masterpieces. He has created us anew in Christ Jesus, so we can do the good things He planned for us long ago."
(Ephesians 2:10)

I ripped open the box from the mail order company to inspect the fun things I had been waiting for—note cards, ribbon, wrapping paper and various greeting cards for upcoming birthdays and other special occasions throughout the year.

As usual, the box contained a handful of junk mail advertisements. As I gathered them up to toss in the trash, one slipped from my hand onto the floor and slid halfway under the refrigerator. I quickly glanced at it before dropping it in the wastebasket. Suddenly, I stopped short, realizing the possibilities of that little ad lying on top of the trash. Could this be the answer to my prayers?

The emotional and physical changes of midlife were forcing themselves on me. Part of my struggle also included the fact that in a few months I would have an empty nest for the first time in thirty years. I accustomed myself to my two older children being out on their own, but I wasn't ready to let go of my youngest child just yet. Sandy had only a few months of high school left and was already preparing for college. *What am I going to do with my life when she is away at school?* I asked myself.

My job was not the answer. It was just that—a job. It provided a paycheck, but it did not bring me satisfaction or fulfillment. I tried various ministries in the church – faith sharing with high school students, singing in the choir, working with the community food pantry, and reading the Bible to the elderly at an assisted-living facility. Although these activities are all good, I knew they weren't enough to fill the void. I needed something bigger, something to devote my life to, something that could fill the empty space in my heart. I didn't know what I was looking for, but I did know I hadn't found it yet.

And so, I began asking God to show me what he wanted for my life. I prayed for something to give my heart and soul to. Now, here I was, possibly holding the answer in my hands—an advertisement for a correspondence course in creative writing.

The ad ignited a spark inside me, and I felt the urge to pursue it. English compositions and essays in high school hardly qualified me as a writer, however. In fact, being a writer never occurred to me, but the ad intrigued me enough to answer. I sent in a sample paragraph, suspecting no one would be turned away no matter how bad the writing might be. I passed, just as I expected, and was eligible for the program.

The skeptic in me, however, believed this was too good to be true. It must be a scam. I checked out the references, and much to my surprise, the organization was a reputable member of its local Chamber of Commerce. By now, the excitement began building inside me. Then came the bottom line—the cost of the course.

It was expensive even with spreading the payments out over the three-year duration of the program. I felt certain my husband would never agree to spending that amount of money, but now that I had gone this far I had to take the final step.

I prepared my little argument to persuade him, pointing out all the benefits of the classes, the potential for earning money in the future and this being the direction I felt God was leading me. I barely got the words out when he surprised me and said, "Go for it!"

The writing course became the turning point in my life. I devoured the lessons and completed it in two years instead of the usual three. It took a few more years of trial, error and rejections before an article of mine was actually published, but little by little, God opened doors for me and provided many opportunities to share my newly acquired gift.

In following His lead, today I am the editor and publisher of a woman's quarterly publication which has provided me with more joy and satisfaction than I ever dreamed possible. Had the ad for the correspondence writing course not dropped to the floor that day, none of this might have happened.

The daughter who left such an empty space in my life has also begun writing. It is my special blessing and privilege to be the publisher of her first article.

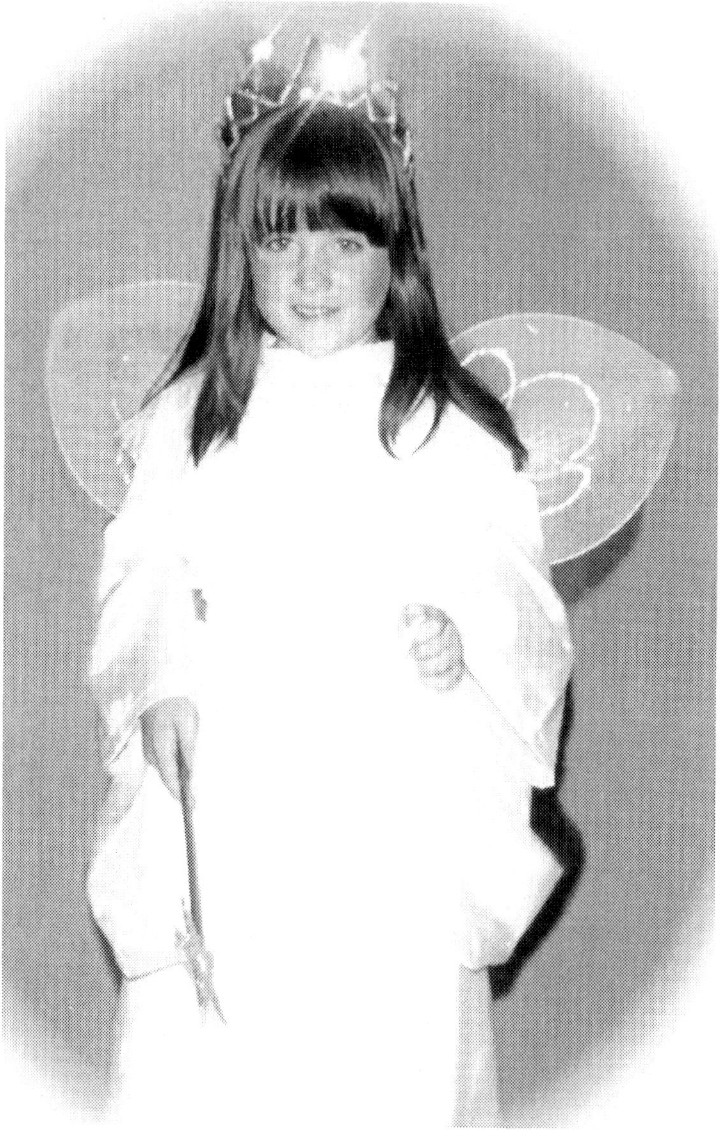

Mary Told Me— Susie's OK

Rosemarie Gortler
As told by Connie Fuller

*"Let the word of Christ dwell in you richly, as you teach and admonish
one another in all wisdom, and as you sing psalms and hymns and
spiritual songs with thankfulness in your hearts to God."
(3 Colossians 12:16)*

"God, I'm not talking to you right now," I sobbed, angrily pointing my finger up at Him. I prayed aloud, choking on tears, "Oh Mary. You're a mom who lost your child. You know the pain I feel." My throat was tight as my sobbing became louder.

Kneeling at my daughter's gravesite, I begged, "Mary, I have to know that Susie is O.K. I have to know that Susie is O.K."

I repeated these words over and over, begging and sobbing—as a plea to our Mother, Mary. I begged the mother of Jesus to comfort me—to lessen the steady gnawing ache that makes you go through the motions of living without feeling alive.

That was a Friday in October, seven months after the unexpected, sudden death of Susie, one of my seven-year-old twin daughters. Barely functioning, I usually got through only the daily motions of caring for my sons and my seven-year-old daughter. Today, the pain wouldn't stop.

Praying at the cemetery sometimes gave small, temporary comfort but that day the pain just intensified. I felt overwhelmed, confused, alone and abandoned.

Seeking solace but still sobbing, I left the cemetery and drove in the direction of my friend, Nancy's house. I knew that her Bible study group was there. I wasn't sure I wanted to hear about God but I had to do something—I had to be with someone. The lump in my throat made it hard to swallow. I drove slowly with tears still falling, the lump in my throat still there and still angry with God. I was still pleading with Mary to let me know that Susie was O.K.

It didn't feel right to be angry with God, but somehow in my mixed up thoughts I believed that Mary would plead my case. As a mother, she would understand how I felt and Jesus would hear her. Somehow, I got through the day and the night.

~~~

The phone rang early the next morning. My practical, organized, not-given-to emotionalism friend, Betsy was calling from Little Rock. She and her husband, Scott had become new parents about the time of Susie's death. I hadn't seen Betsy in quite a while.

"Connie, this is Betsy. Something happened that I have to tell you about. Scott didn't want me to call you because he said it might upset you but I knew I had to tell you."

She hesitated, and then began again. " I had a dream last night. Susie was with me—we were the only two in the house." She went on, "It was dark. Susie and I walked down the hallway. I was fumbling for a light switch to let the two dogs out. I couldn't find it. We opened the front door. The moon was bright and everything outside was light. The dream was so vivid."

Betsy continued, "I told Susie to stay inside and I'd walk the dogs. I walked the dogs, lost sight of one and turned to talk to Susie—but she wasn't there."

"I called out to Susie, asking where she was because I couldn't see her. She had disappeared into the space that was dark. She answered me in a loud, clear voice telling me that she was right there. I repeated that I couldn't see her."

Betsy said that Susie answered twice, *"Just tell my mommy that I'm O.K."*—again in a loud, clear voice—*and I knew that I had to tell you she was O.K."*

Betsy went on to describe awakening about midnight in a cold sweat. "I knew it was a dream but different from any dream I've ever had. I felt compelled to tell you what Susie said."

"I have to know that Susie is OK," was my prayer to Mary.

~~~

A little later that morning, my strong Christian Bible study friend called. I wanted to tell her about Betsy's dream but she stopped me, saying, "Let me tell you my story first." She explained that she awakened at one o'clock in the morning with a strong need to pray for Connie's peace and comfort. She told me that she got out of bed, knelt down and prayed for a long while.

~~~

One o'clock Eastern Standard Time is twelve o'clock in Little Rock—*Nancy was praying as Betsy was dreaming.* I knew that my Mary heard my prayer –and answered it.

I apologized to Jesus and I thanked Mary. The pain of losing Susie will never go away but I knew peace and I was comforted. I can go on to care for my other children.

I know Susie is OK. Jesus and Mary told me so.

Chocolate Pie with the Funny Crust

Sallie Bachar

When I was a young, stay-at-home Mom and counting calories was not an issue, I let each child take a turn picking his or her favorite dessert for me to make. My four-year-old daughter, Terri, always asked for "the pie with the funny crust." Of course, she only scooped out the filling and never ate the crust.

Silky Chocolate Pie with Meringue Crust

Crust: 2 egg whites
Pinch of salt
Pinch of cream of tartar
½ teaspoon vanilla
7 tablespoons sugar

Filling: ½ cup butter or margarine
½ cup sugar
2 oz. unsweetened chocolate
1 teaspoon vanilla
2 eggs, unbeaten

Prepare crust. Beat egg whites until frothy. Add salt and cream of tartar. Continue beating until stiff. Add vanilla and sugar, one tablespoon at a time, continuing to beat until stiff peaks form. Spread in a greased pie pan, forming a shell, and bake at 275 degrees for 1 hour. Turn off heat and leave in oven 30 minutes longer. Let cool before adding filling.

Prepare filling. Cream butter in mixing bowl. Gradually add sugar, creaming well. Blend in chocolate and vanilla. Add eggs, one at a time, beating 3-5 minutes after each. Spoon into cooled shell and chill 2 hours.

We teach our children how to work together and how to pray together.

Paul's Joy

Rosemarie Gortler

"Even though I walk through the valley of the shadow of death, I fear no evil; for Thou art with me; Thy rod and Thy staff they comfort me." (Psalm 23:4)

Ugh! New Year's Eve again!

My husband and I really dislike the usual New Year's Eve partying. Maybe it challenges the peace and quiet joy of Christmastime—even in our noisy, grandchild filled home. The parties seem so *forced*—like compulsory fun.

When we learned that New Year's Eve Mass was being offered at church, followed by breakfast in the church "activity center" it sounded like a perfect alternative. *That's* how we would usher in the New Year.

Following an inspirational first Mass of the year, we proceeded to the activity center for breakfast. Two old friends, Paul and Rosalie, sat next to us. We hadn't seen them in months and were delighted with an opportunity to catch up. In August of 1995, Paul was diagnosed with Merkel's cell cancer, a rare and fatal type of cancer. He had been experiencing up and down periods but the last words we heard had been that Paul was in remission—doing quite well.

That night, he looked terrific—surprisingly healthy and robust. The big grin, together with the loss of hair from treatments, gave him the Yul Brenner look. He responded to teasing about looking handsome and sexy with a dimpled, posed smile.

I asked how things were going. Paul grinned again, "About six months ago I was given three months to live. Funny thing—I feel good now. Don't look so sad. I'm at peace and this whole thing could be joyous if I didn't have to leave Rosie behind. I feel like a kid waiting for Christmas. I think I'm at peace with the Lord and I'm telling my story to anyone who will listen. Believe it or not, I've been helping people straighten out their lives as I come to the end of mine."

Rosie smiled a sad smile. It was clear that her feelings about Paul dying were very different from his. I could almost see her thoughts about the coming year and the sadness she would have to cope with—one more time. They had lost their grown son two years before, after a lengthy illness. Faith and their love for each other carried them through that sadness. Soon Paul would be gone. How would she cope without him?

~~~

My thoughts flashed back to visiting Paul at the hospital shortly after his diagnosis and surgery. He had a lot of hope and his expectation was that he would overcome all obstacles and be cured. Within a short period, the cancer caused pain and other symptoms, the worst of which was an acutely distorted sense of smell and taste that permeated his every breath. Food tasted terrible. Everything smelled bad enough to physically upset him. I remember Rosie telling us how frustrated she was at her inability to help him. "I don't know what to do. He can't even tolerate the smell of clean sheets on the bed!"

Discouraged and angry with God, Paul worked at accepting his prognosis—but not his imminent death. He bargained first for time and prayed that he at least be physically comfortable and in good humor for his family and friends. His doctor prescribed medication to help calm the agony of distorted taste and smell problems, but within two days, the medication precipitated a deep depression. Paul's mood shifted severely. He became agitated, hostile and demanding at home and in the office. A short course of an antidepressant quickly reversed this, allowing him to return to the work he loved and to the clients he served—some for more than thirty years. He was feeling more comfortable.

Paul believed his prayers were answered. He had lots more energy. He threw himself into his work and his good humor was restored. Problems with taste and smell were minimized and tolerable. His energy level was high and even the pain became tolerable. He knew he was not healed.

He began telling clients about his illness, about how he prayed for extra time and for physical comfort and how he was soon scheduled to "go home." Paul reminded them—"you don't know when your time is up" and how grateful he was to have this time to prepare. People he had not seen since the onset of his illness called to ask him to lunch so that he might verify what they heard from others. Cards kept coming, most with notes that

Paul's message sent them back to church and to God. Friends thought Paul was in long-term remission. He knew he was not and spoke about God's goodness in allowing him the extended time he prayed for.

~~~

My attention turned back to Paul and Rosie. Paul glowed. He wanted to talk, but the look on Rosie's face made it hard to continue. We invited them to lunch the following week including Rosie in the invitation—somehow knowing that he would come alone. Paul readily accepted, laughing as he commented that he had never in his life had so many luncheon invitations. "I get invited out almost every day and it's because people really want to talk about God."

~~~

Paul did come alone. Two of our grandsons were visiting us for the weekend and he wanted them to hear what he had to say, too. In fact, he was primarily addressing the children as he emphasized "... the more I look back on life, the more I see God's hand guiding it." Paul heard the younger grandson whisper to me, "Nana, it sounds like he wants to die!"

Paul smiled as he explained that he *didn't* want to die, but that he *did* want to live with God and to have the eternal happiness that Jesus died to give us. Paul went on to add that he didn't want to leave his wife, whom he loved more than anything on earth, or to leave the rest of his family but he was ready because he believed he was being called. "It's why we were born in the first place."

The children listened intently as Paul described how sorry he felt for himself when he was first diagnosed. "I kept saying— Why me, Lord??? I was afraid. I became very depressed and I prayed hard for a miracle—to be cured. Instead, God kept putting me in touch with people who were hungry to hear about Him. I had a lot of pain and the treatments made me lose my sense of taste and smell. I was even arrested because the medication they gave me made me woozy, and I was picked up for drunk driving—and God sent me more people who wanted to hear about Him. He keeps sending them."

Paul continued, "I found myself being comforted as I helped others. Slowly, I was coming to the realization that I am going home to Him. I stopped trying to diminish or delete pain. I use pain because I think it has a purpose." Paul described the paradoxical twists and turns of life since his illness began—then paused for a moment before saying that it just occurred to him that his life was full of God working on him through paradoxes.

He was the fourth of five children—raised in the Dutch Reform Church—questioning everything and everybody. "I married Catholic Rosie and I argued with priests about mortal and venial sin. I argued about everything and then I converted to Catholicism at 21 years old." We had to chuckle as he mimicked his past argumentative behaviors.

Following a lunch that can only be described as prayerfully exciting, Paul left. The children asked about him from time to time. They seemed to remember his message well but because he was doing so much better, they believed Paul was cured. Paul made going to live with Jesus so inviting that I was careful to emphasize to them that you only go when called.

Paul's condition worsened slowly as spring approached. He was offering up more pain than he ever imagined having. Rosie speaks of him as uncomplaining. She recalls him sitting up in bed—with a smile on his face—reminding her, "It won't be long now." Recognizing the pain he felt, she sat behind him, with her head on his shoulder and arms encircling his waist. "I told him that I wanted him to go with the angels when they came for him, and that I would meet him someday." Paul responded with a simple, "O.K."

He died that night, July 17, 1998.

~~~

Paul's struggle with life and death is repeated by many others, many times every day—prayers, faith, physical suffering—shared by millions of terminally ill people all over the world. I was inspired by the way Paul used dying to reach out and give glory to God.

Paul left a lengthy letter to be read by our priest at his viewing. The letter spoke of the growth of his faith over the many months and the joy he felt because his Christmas finally arrived. He asked that no one grieve for him and shared a story he read many months before that went to the heart of our faith. The story as Paul recalled it:

One Christmas Eve in a farming area, a man was at home when his family had gone to Midnight Mass. He had chosen not to go because he could not accept the idea that God would become Man and dwell among us. It didn't make any sense to him.

As he was seated and reading, a violent winter storm blew up with heavy winds and heavy snow. He heard a thump against his window. He got up, looked out and saw that a bird had flown into his window and was lying on the porch. He saw that there was a whole flock of birds. He knew that many of these birds would die or be lost to the storm if they could not find shelter.

The man bundled up and went out to open the barn doors hoping that the birds would see their salvation and fly inside. The birds did not understand what he was trying to do and were afraid. He ran out into the yard—got behind them, waving his arms, jumping up and down—yelling for them to fly into the open barn doors—to no avail. He went back to the barn and stood in the open doors, wondering what he could do to make them follow him. The thought came to him that if only he could become a bird, he could lead them all to safety.

The weight of his thought came crashing in on him and he understood why God had to become man. He fell to his knees and wept.

Paul ended his letter with loving words to his dearest Rosie and a wish for all of us to find the Peace of Christ.
There was a long silence following the reading, followed by a soft buzzing of voices sharing how Paul's death touched their faith!

God answered Paul's prayers by giving him extra time, by comforting him and by preparing him for eternity with Him. Paul answered God's call by comforting those whom God sent to be comforted. I thank God for the way He used Paul to comfort and inspire many of us. I thank Paul for the memorable messages he gave to my grandsons.

I'm sure there are others like Paul—but I was a witness to Paul's response to God. I'm not as distressed at the thought of dying as I was before talking to Paul. I pray I can live my death as joyously and expectantly as Paul did.

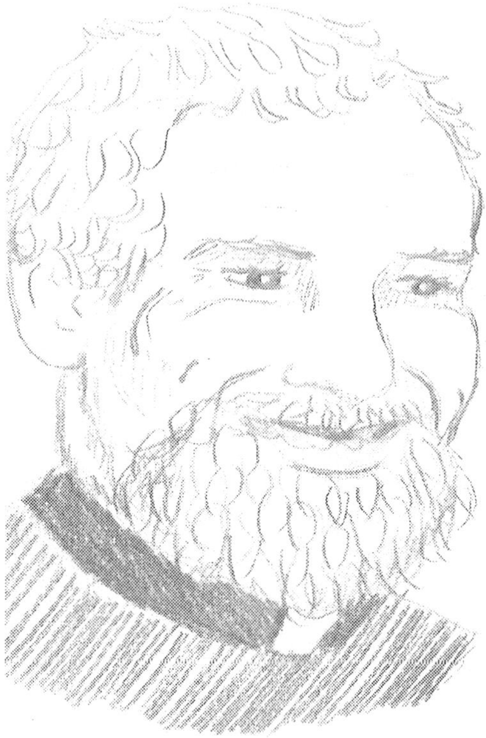

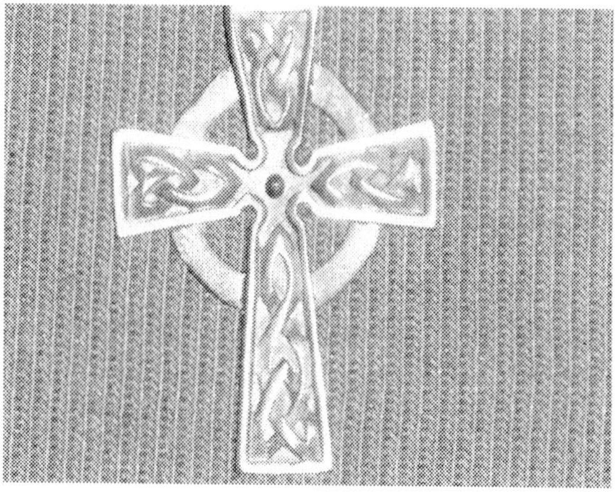

Elizabeth and the Irish Priest

Rosemarie Gortler
As told by Ellen and Fred Gortler

"Blessed are they who mourn, for they shall be comforted."
(Matthew 5:4)

Time usually fades the memory of a face seen once, more than 20 years ago. But, the face, the voice and the words of the Irish priest who came to comfort us following my wife, Ellen's, miscarriage is as clear, vivid and unforgettable as it was the day we met him.

We were a young military family, so when Ellen began cramping and bleeding, we rushed to Bethesda Naval Hospital. The military doctor who came to examine her couldn't have been much older than we were. He casually told us told us that Ellen was having a spontaneous abortion. Confused, hurt and angry, we responded emotionally to the ugly "abortion" word until he explained that this meant she was already having a miscarriage. He added that a surgical procedure was necessary.

I asked to see a Catholic chaplain before any surgical procedure was performed. The doctor promised to relay my request and returned to say that there was no Catholic Chaplain at the base at this time, but that the duty chaplain would be in to see us. Military chaplains are well versed in all religions—so we gratefully accepted the offer. Ellen was grieving our loss and I felt so helpless to comfort her—or even to comfort myself. There isn't much you can say when you are both so sad. You try to help each other, but all you can do is cling together. Many people do not understand that the loss of an unborn child is a very real death and that parents grieve and mourn the death of their unborn child.

Within minutes, a short, stout Irish priest came into her room. His beard was bushy, he had a thick Irish brogue and a heart as big as Texas—seemingly straight out of central casting for a Hollywood movie. Father put us at ease almost immediately. He shared his family history, "of eleven brothers and sisters—all nuns and priests, except for the one who went from our mother's womb straight to Heaven". We smiled when he added that his mother told the ten siblings that she hoped they would all be as successful as that sister who got to heaven.

~~~

The staff arrived to take Ellen into the surgical unit. They wheeled her out and I was left to pace, fidget and sigh. Father stayed with me the whole time, giving comfort and kind words. He was still there when Ellen returned, a bit groggy but coherent and sad.

~~~

When Ellen was more awake, Father asked what we would have named our baby. Believing that we lost a son, I replied, "Fred, to honor my father."

"No," he responded, "this baby is a girl." He didn't explain further but went on, "May I suggest that we honor St. Elizabeth of Hungary since this is her feast day?" He gave us no time to respond and began to pray and to baptize Elizabeth's tissue, which was obtained during the surgical procedure. We wondered how he could know that our baby was a girl but we didn't ask any questions.

Feeling exhausted, yet comforted, by this wonderful priest's words and prayers, Ellen rested and then fell sleep. We went home the next day—without carrying our baby girl in our arms. We remembered Father's words—that she would always be our baby girl, though not living here on earth. It didn't take away the sadness, but it was a comforting reminder.

We were indebted to this priest who made our loss a bit more bearable. I picked up a "thank you" card and a small memento and went to the hospital to tell him how grateful we were for his prayers, for baptizing Elizabeth and for his caring support.

The senior chaplain came out and apologized for not having a Catholic chaplain on duty when we needed one. I told him what happened and how Father's presence and prayers provided so much comfort. He looked surprised. I described the priest by his unique appearance, his name and his brogue. The chaplain looked more and more surprised, then confused. He explained that there was no one on staff who looked like that or spoke with a brogue and repeated that there was no Catholic chaplain at the hospital on base the night Ellen miscarried. He could not explain the happenings of the previous night. However, he assured us that the man who came was not part of their staff.

I went home confused. Ellen was confused. We decided that God had embraced us that night because of our prayers and because we so needed help to get through our sorrow.

Was Father an Angel? If so, it was hard to accept that we were special enough to warrant an angelic appearance. But since that time, we have discovered that many people have had equally inexplicable experiences. We know now that it isn't that we are special. It is because our God is so special and because God is always there when we fervently ask for His help.

~~~

It is 24 years later. Our oldest daughter, Julie, is married and pregnant. I was recently sent on work travel to Omaha, Nebraska. During my alone times, I thought of Julie and began remembering the birth of each of our children. I especially remembered Elizabeth and the Irish priest.

On the Sunday of my travel, I went to Mass at a church that reminded me of my childhood parish. I found literature on St.

Elizabeth of Hungary and smiled when I read that among her other causes, St. Elizabeth is the patron saint of children who die. Twenty-five years had passed since our experience at the naval hospital. But I was humbled at how the priest on duty that night carried us when we could not walk on our own.

The full extent of that evening and the blessings given us have been vividly replayed in my and Ellen's memories. And, why, when we recall every single, other detail, can't we recall Father's name?

God reveals a bit at a time—or maybe we can only process His love and support a bit at a time. I only know that we are very loved by our God.

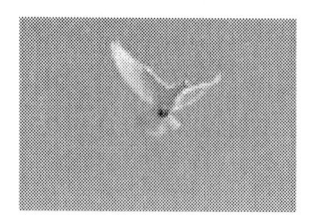

Baked Fudge Pudding Cake

Diane Carroll Vogel

Children like me who grew up in the forties and fifties were used to home cooked meals, including desserts. Desserts that involved warm pudding and rich chocolate were special treats. So, I searched through my recipe files for mouth-watering chocolate desserts that were family favorites, like Baked Fudge Pudding Cake. The delicious aroma of this scrumptious cake as it baked always carried me back to Mom's kitchen in the 1950's.

And my mouth always watered and stomach growled in eager anticipation of this gooey, chocolaty delight.

Baked Fudge Pudding Cake

1 cup sifted all-purpose flour
2 teaspoons baking powder
½ teaspoon salt
½ cup sugar
2 tablespoons cocoa
½ cup chopped nuts
½ cup milk
1 teaspoon vanilla
2 tablespoons melted shortening

Sift together the flour, baking powder, salt, sugar and cocoa.

Stir in the nuts, milk, vanilla, and melted shortening. Spread the batter in a greased, 8-inch square pan.

Pour the topping over the batter. Bake in moderate (350 degree) oven for 35-40 minutes.

For topping combine ¼ cup cocoa and ¾ cup brown sugar. Stir in 1 ¾ cup hot water.

Thank you, Lord, for the delights of comfort food and happy memories.

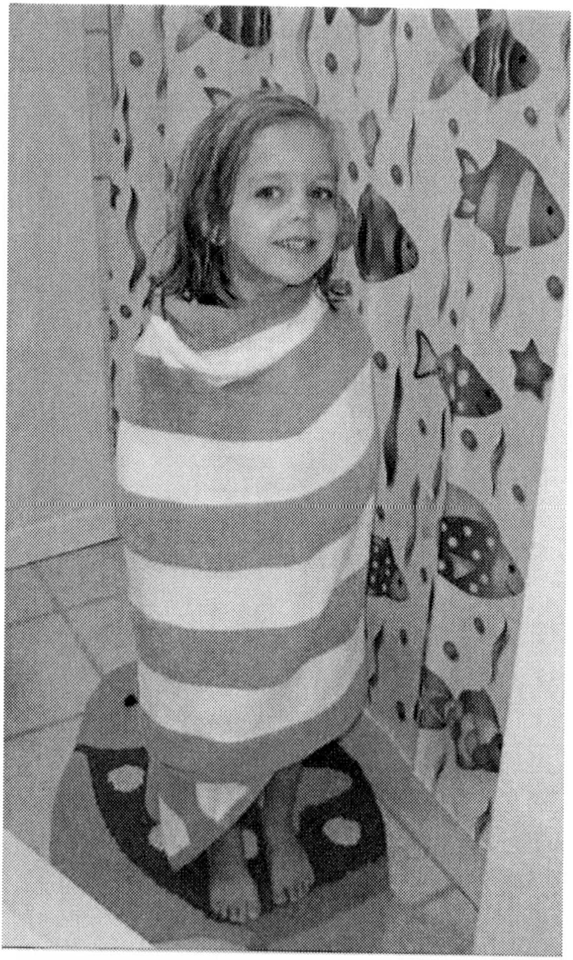

Wrapped in Prayer

Diane Carroll Vogel

"Truly you have formed my inmost being; You knit me in my Mother's womb. I give You thanks that I am fearfully, wonderfully made; wonderful are Your works."
(Psalm 139:13-14)

One winter evening years ago, I was playing in the bathtub while my mother was getting my bed and pajamas ready. She told me she would be back in a couple of minutes, cautioning me not to touch the taps.

For a four-year-old, a few minutes can seem an eternity, and when the water started turning lukewarm, I grew impatient. I turned on the faucet full blast. *Maybe* I felt guilty about disobeying Mommy, but that warm water sure felt good—at least for a few moments! In those days, water tanks emptied quickly and reheated slowly, and soon only cold water streamed from the faucet.

Shivering and sobbing, I was sure I would be in big trouble for touching those taps. At this point, my mother—who had probably been gone for only minutes—walked into the bathroom.

"Oh my," she cried. Scooping me up, she wrapped me in a big fluffy towel and hugged me until my shaking subsided. Instead of scolding me, she enfolded me in her comforting love.

That childhood memory of my mother's caring embrace came to mind when my friend, Wren, told me about the Prayer Shawl Ministry she helped organize. Shawl ministries can be found nationwide, and usually those involved knit or crochet shawls for people who are experiencing difficulties in their lives.

Sometimes, shawls are also given for joyous occasions such as weddings, births and ordinations.

The crafters, who pray throughout the creation of their shawls, see their ministry as a way to share the love of Christ with those in need. After the shawl is completed, it is often given a final, special blessing before being sent on its way. The shawls offer solace, like the warmth of a mother's hug, wrapping the person in a comforting embrace.

Wren also told me a remarkable story about her neighbor, who was given one of her group's prayer shawls. This man had sustained severe injuries in an automobile accident. Hospitalization and rehabilitation followed, yet within two months, Wren saw him walking in the neighborhood with his wife.

Wren went outside to say hello, and commented on his amazing progress. He told her he attributed his quick recovery to the prayer shawl he was given and the spiritual support of family and friends. Wren added that her neighbor's pastor calls him "Miracle Man!"

There is a sweet side note to this story. When another member of this ministry, also a neighbor of the injured man, was picking out a shawl for him, her eyes were drawn to a small one in pink. She knew the man's young daughter was distraught over what had happened to her daddy and needed consolation. The pink shawl was the perfect choice.

This was the *only* pink shawl available, and in fact, this group rarely makes any in that shade. When the child saw the shawl, her face lit up. She wrapped herself in its soft folds and exclaimed, "Pink is my favorite color!" Through the Prayer Shawl Ministry, the Lord had indeed extended love and comfort to both father and child!

My sister, Marilyn, who suffers from excruciatingly painful and frequent back spasms, was also blessed with one of the Prayer Shawl Ministry's beautiful creations. After deliberating over a large selection of shawls in assorted styles and colors, I selected one in a soothing green color to send to her for her birthday. Wren told me that "just the right" shawl always seems to be on hand to suit the special needs of a recipient, and this certainly was true in Marilyn's case.

The pamphlet that accompanied my sister's shawl included the following message: "May God's grace be upon this shawl—warming, comforting, enfolding and embracing. May you be cradled in hope, kept in joy, graced with peace, and wrapped in love."

Marilyn wrote in appreciation: "I just love the prayer shawl. What a great idea. I can use it even in the summer. Sometimes when I wake up at night with a spasm and sit on the edge of the bed, the air conditioner is on. The cold draft makes things worse. I have often ended up grabbing my heavy bathrobe and pulling it sideways around my shoulders like a shawl. Obviously, I do the same thing in the winter when I wake up and the heat is turned down for the night.

I never thought of a shawl, but it seems the perfect solution to a lot of my problems. I can use it in the car or in my chair. And by the way, the color is beautiful and it does feel so soft and comforting. I can't thank you enough." When Marilyn was hospitalized recently with pneumonia, she brought her prayer shawl with her as a source of warmth and solace.

Prayer and faith wrap us in God's love. So do those who minister to us when we are in need of comfort, and celebrate with us on joyous occasions.

"Come. You have my Father's blessing! Inherit the kingdom prepared for you from the creation of the world. For I was hungry and you gave me food, I was thirsty and you gave me drink. I was a stranger and you welcomed me, naked and you clothed me. I was ill and you comforted me, in prison and you came to visit me."

Matthew 26:34-36

Prayer, Faith and a Bit of Chocolate

Anastasia and Nana, God's Rescue Squad

Rosemarie Gortler
As told by Marigrace Chakwin

"See, I am sending an angel before you, to guard you on the way and bring you to the place I have prepared."
(Exodus 23: 20-23)

My story sounds unbelievable! If it didn't happen to me, I would have trouble believing it, but honestly, it's as factual as the sun coming up every morning!

My sister, Judi, and I were married at a double wedding, and our firstborn children were boys, born four days apart and, delivered by the same doctor at the same hospital. Because she had a C-Section before I delivered, her hospital stay was longer than mine. We shared a double hospital room for three days. This, of course was when mom and baby were cared for in the hospital for several days—before the current practice of "drive through baby delivery."

Judi and I were close friends as well as sisters, and living in the same town was great. We could get together often, go shopping, and do all that sister stuff that is so special. When she had to move some 700 miles away, I really missed her and she missed me, my other sister and our brothers. To be truthful, she sounded sad and a bit lonely whenever we talked on the phone.

You can imagine how excited I was at the thought of visiting her over the Easter break after their move. It was going to be a special time and I wanted to make her a special gift. I decided on a framed counted cross-stitch piece for her kitchen. Judi was into country décor and I found just the right size pattern of dressed up country goose in a perfect color arrangement. I worked on it every spare minute and it was finished in time to take to the Ben Franklin store to purchase the material to frame my masterpiece. I was anticipating Judi's enthusiastic reaction to my surprise. I was elated.

With my children in tow and an armful of "stuff" that mothers carry around, I took my completed craft to choose the foam board, mat and frame that I would use to finish the piece. I returned home and put the bag on the counter.

~~~

It was hard to delay framing my country goose that afternoon. It was time to tend to those mother tasks—fix dinner, eat dinner, clean the kitchen, bathe the children, say prayers and tuck the children in. Finally, tasks all completed, I sat down to frame my masterpiece.

But—the counted cross-stitch piece was missing from the bag that held the framing material. Dumping out the contents and going through whatever I had with me at Ben Franklin produced nothing. I looked in the bag again. Nothing! The piece was gone. It was too late to go back to the store.

Sadly, I went to bed, determined to be at the store tomorrow the minute it opened.

~~~

I prayed hard that I would find my work. Our family names our Guardian Angels and I often talk to Anastasia, my guardian angel. After prayers and before falling asleep, I asked my Anastasia to please help me find Judi's surprise.

During the night, I dreamed of my grandmother. Nana, as we called her, was devoted to all of us. She wanted us to be as close to our siblings as she was to hers. In my dream, Nana told me to look in the trashcan to the right of and behind the counter at Ben Franklin to find my counted cross-stitch. The dream was so real—so vivid. I could hardly wait for the day to begin. I was that sure that I would find my country goose.

~~~

The next day was Sunday and the store didn't open until noon. Right after church, I rushed in and asked the clerk if anyone had found my counted cross-stitch and turned it in. She assured me it wasn't there. I asked her to check the trashcan and she replied that all trashcans had been emptied the night before. I was willing to "dumpster dive" to find the piece, but first needed to check where my Nana had told me to look. I asked her to check the trashcans at all of the registers and she did a quick look inside each, telling me emphatically that all the cans were empty.

I asked her to **please** check the trashcan on the right, which was set farther back. She sighed and again repeated, "The cans are emptied every night." Nevertheless, she did walk over and look into the trashcan. She lifted the can, and there was only a crumpled plastic store bag in the bottom. When she took out the bag, there was my counted cross-stitch country goose! I could have cried with joy and gratitude. The clerk's eyes were wide with amazement.

How and why did this happen? I don't know, but I know that Anastasia has been active in my life and that Nana was certainly in the picture somehow. She was so good to all of us and wanted us to love and please each other. It reminds me of God and how He wants us to love each other, to do for each other.

God does give us everyday miracles which we erroneously call luck. I think my Guardian Angel, Anastasia, prayed for this to happen and God used Nana, who loves me and who I would trust to help me to relieve my sister's "moving away" sadness.

A Final Quick Chocolate Fix

Place a couple of teaspoons—or tablespoons—of your favorite canned or boxed chocolate frosting in the microwave for a few seconds until melted.

Pour over any fresh or canned fruit and add a dollop of whipped cream or non- dairy whipped topping and enjoy the delight of the quickest fix imaginable.

The Best Recipe of All

Pray a lot.

Have Faith in our God because He is always there for us.

Enjoy the beauty of His simple gifts, including sweet and comforting bits of chocolate.

Be aware of the everyday miracles in your own life—and give praise and thanks to God for them!

Rosemarie, Diane and Sallie

Acknowledgements
The following stories have been previously published.

"Laura's Gift" was published in the March, 1998 issue of *The St. Anthony Messenger*.

"Wake-up Call" was published in the September-October, 1998 issue of *Women Alive*!

"A Mother's Undying Love" was published under the title "Of Santa, a Seamstress and a Silver Spoon" in December, 2008 in *Town and County* magazine of *The Free Lance-Star*.

"Mary Told Me—Susie's O.K." was published in the March-April, 2000 issue of *Queen of All Hearts*.

"Paul's Joy" was published in the February, 2001 issue of *The St. Anthony Messenger*.

The authors would like to thank Mimi Sternhagen for designing and illustrating the cover of *Prayer, Faith and a Bit of Chocolate*. They would also like to thank their husbands, Fred Gortler, Tom Vogel and Ted Bachar for their support during the countless hours they spent on their computers.

Authors

Rosemarie Gortler, a Licensed Professional Counselor, is a freelance writer who has been published in *The St. Anthony Messenger* and other periodicals. She is also the co-author of a five-volume religious book series for children published by *Our Sunday Visitor*.

The Ten Commandments for Children, the fourth in that series, *was a 2008 second place award winner* from the Catholic Press Association of the United States and Canada.

Diane Carroll Vogel, a retired English teacher, is a freelance writer who has won awards from the Virginia Press Women and National Federation of Press Women. Her articles have appeared in *Pauses*, the *Virginia English Bulletin* published by the Virginia Association of Teachers of English Language Arts, and *Town & County* magazine published by *The Free Lance-Star*.

Sallie Bachar is the author of *Autumn Gold- a Season of Hope*. She is a freelance writer and a journalist for the Catholic Herald of Superior Wisconsin. Sallie is also the editor of a quarterly publication, *Pauses... An Oasis for Today's Catholic Woman*. Her work has appeared in *Liguorian* and other Christian Publications.

Rosemarie and Sallie met at a Writers' Workshop in Wisconsin, Sallie's home state. Diane and Rosemarie live in the same Virginia neighborhood and are members of their church Women's Guild.

Prayer, Faith and a Bit of Chocolate came about because of the women's growing friendship, a collective desire to share stories of everyday miracles, and a fondness for chocolate.